HUSBAND
AND
WIFE

"With three things my spirit is pleased, which are approved before God and men: The concord of brethren, and the love of neighbors, and man and wife that agree well together."

—Ecclesiasticus 25:1-2

HUSBAND
AND
WIFE

THE JOYS, SORROWS AND
GLORIES OF MARRIED LIFE

By

Father Paul A. Wickens

<small>SECOND EDITION</small>

*"And God created man to his own image:
to the image of God he created him: male
and female he created them. And God blessed
them, saying: Increase and multiply, and fill
the earth, and subdue it."*
    —Genesis 1:27-28

TAN BOOKS AND PUBLISHERS, INC.
Rockford, Illinois 61105

Library of Congress Catalog Card No.: 98-61686

ISBN 0-89555-645-6

Cover design by Peter Massari. Photo of Timothy and Melissa Gardner at their June 13, 1998 wedding, on the Feast of St. Anthony of Padua.

Rev. Paul A. Wickens was ordained in 1955 at Sacred Heart Cathedral in Newark, New Jersey. His mailing address is St. Anthony of Padua Chapel, 1360 Pleasant Valley Way, West Orange, New Jersey 07052.

Printed and bound in the United States of America.

TAN BOOKS AND PUBLISHERS, INC.
P.O. Box 424
Rockford, Illinois 61105
2000

THE NUPTIAL BLESSING

MAY the God of Abraham, the God of Isaac, and the God of Jacob be with you, and may He fulfill His blessing in you: that you may see your children's children even to the third and fourth generation, and thereafter may you have life everlasting, by the grace of Our Lord Jesus Christ, who with the Father and the Holy Ghost liveth and reigneth, God forever and ever. Amen.

—From the Nuptial Mass of the Traditional Roman Liturgy

CONTENTS

Publisher's Preface. ix

Foreword xi

1. The Priest as Marriage Instructor 1

2. Marriage Today 3

3. The Positive Side of Marriage:
   God and Marriage 17

4. Togetherness, or The Union of Mind and Heart
   (Differences between Male and Female). . . 30

5. The Physical Union. 49

Appendix 1
   Periodic Continence. 73

Appendix 2
   Reflections 81

Appendix 3
   Prayer to the Most Sacred Heart of Jesus . . 83

PUBLISHER'S PREFACE

The title, or even the subtitle, of this book might well be *The Catholic View of Marriage* because, in a capsule form, that is what the book is about. Yes, "The *Catholic* View of Marriage," for certainly the Catholic Church has a number of fundamental and far-reaching teachings on the nature and purpose of marriage, the role of *husband and wife* within a Catholic marriage and the place of the children—such that Catholic marriage, properly practiced, differs in a number of ways from the practices current in non-sacramental marriages and even from those of marriages between baptized non-Catholic Christians.

The duties and obligations of each spouse toward the other within a Catholic marriage, the marital morality they must observe, the proper relationship of the woman to the man regarding headship within the marriage, the responsibility of that headship on the man, the need for the woman to be primarily homemaker and mother, the understood indissolubility of marriage—all these Catholic norms (and others) only help to promote true harmony and increased love between the spouses and a sense of security for the children. In effect, these Catholic norms help produce happy marriages.

Scores of Catholic books on marriage have been written in the last 75 years, proving that Catholic marriage is indeed a fertile subject for Catholic writers. And of all such books that I know about, the most telling title ever given any of them was *Why Catholic Marriage Is Different*. That was probably far from the best *book* on Catholic marriage, but it probably had the best title by far, because in those five simple words it announces to the reader that Catholic marriage *is indeed* different from non-Catholic marriage. And Fr. Paul Wickens' excellent little book, *Husband and Wife*, will amply show the reader why.

In brief, why? Because—in brief—Catholic marriage is illuminated by the Divine Revelation of Jesus Christ, the God-Man, who came to "give testimony to the truth." (*John* 18:37). Man can discern with his unaided reason the principal lineaments of marriage, but Original Sin and his own personal sins help blind him to the exact truth about marriage and help weaken his will to accept that truth, even when he sees it clearly. But with Divine Revelation shedding its light upon the institution of marriage, "everyone that is of the truth" (*John* 18:37) and willing to accept God's word will see marriage for what it truly is and what it is truly supposed to be.

Catholic marriage, in short, is based upon true principles laid down by Almighty God. And if man will but follow and adhere to these principles, then marriages will be happy, harmonious, fruitful in graces and in children, and will promote the eternal salvation of the spouses and their children and foster the well-being of the Church and of society. In reading this book, therefore, one should rid his mind of all secular notions of marriage and open it to the divine truth regarding this God-given institution in which the majority of human beings are called to work out their salvation.

Thomas A. Nelson
February 27, 1999
St. Gabriel of
    The Sorrowful Mother

FOREWORD

Strangers in Many Ways

At wedding receptions one often hears a song originally recorded by "The Carpenters" entitled "For All We Know":

> *Love, look at the two of us,*
> *Strangers in many ways.*
> *Let's take a lifetime to say,*
> *"I knew you well . . ."*

Yes! Most couples at the time of their marriage are still actually "strangers in many ways." But they need not worry! By *God's grace,* they will *grow together* in love, understanding and holiness.

The purpose of this small book is to help married people understand each other better, to help them with some of the common problems most couples encounter in marriage. It is not intended to be complete, by any means, but it is at least a "good start" to arriving at an understanding of each other and of the state of life they have entered into, what its purpose is and how God expects them to work out their eternal salvation within its realm.

The information and advice contained in this book are really the product of many priests, many counselors and many married couples.

Over a period of thirty-five years, especially through the outlines given to us at (pre-Vatican II) Cana Conferences, we were able to accumulate copious notes on various aspects of the state of marriage, and consequently we are able to pass along the accumulated wisdom of many people on this complex but so very important subject.

Our heartfelt thanks go out to those wonderful Catholic people—some of them now deceased—who through their ideas and advice made this little book possible.

—Fr. Paul A. Wickens
June 13, 1992
Feast of St. Anthony of Padua

HUSBAND
AND
WIFE

"Have you not read, that he who made man from the beginning, made them male and female? And he said: For this cause shall a man leave father and mother, and shall cleave to his wife, and they two shall be in one flesh."

—Matthew 19:4-5

Chapter 1

THE PRIEST AS MARRIAGE INSTRUCTOR

One may ask how a priest might be capable of giving marriage instructions. After all, he is not married. How does he know the joys, the sufferings and the problems in marriage?

To answer this objection, may we point out that a priest is capable because of four factors: 1) his training, 2) his experience, 3) his objectivity and 4) the grace of Holy Orders.

1. His Training: During his minimum of 8 years of college and seminary, he was given a well-rounded education, including an in-depth study of marriage.

2. His Experience: During his lifetime, a priest comes into contact with a countless variety of marriages. He has known newlywed couples as well as golden jubilarians. He sees the young and the old, the rich and the poor. He sees the happy homes and the unhappy homes, the successful marriages and the failed marriages. Thus, whereas the priest does not personally experience the joys and problems of this sacred union, he does obtain a wide understanding about it. One must realize that it is not necessary to experience intimately every phase of life in order to understand people and their situations. Certainly surgeons do not need to have gone through the experience of, let us say, a brain tumor operation in order to understand its ramifications. A client who hires a lawyer does not require that the lawyer have been

convicted of a crime or have spent time in prison.

Personal experience is not the only teacher, and in fact, it is not necessarily the best teacher. For example, criminals often do not learn from the experience of arrest, trial and incarceration. Many fall back into the same crimes despite repeated punishment.

The experience that the priest possesses is vicarious, but richly varied and is buttressed with a knowledge of human nature and a grasp of true religious teaching.

3. His Objectivity: The priest is neither husband nor wife and is able to look at marriage from an objective point of view. He can step back, in effect, to get an overall view of the institution of marriage. One cannot always see the forest because of the trees. That is, when one is caught up in a situation, he or she often loses perspective. A famous monastic once said that in order for him more clearly to understand religious life, he would from time to time walk to a hill about one half mile from the monastery. From that vantage point, he could grasp the whole picture of monastery life and its purpose. Similarly, the priest is able to "step back" and examine the nature of marriage in an objective and detached manner.

4. The grace of Holy Orders: On the day of ordination, a great Sacrament is conferred upon a man. He is given Holy Orders. Not only does this Sacrament elevate Him to the status of Alter Christus— "Another Christ"—but it guarantees him the graces to fulfill the various functions of his state of life. One very important function is to instruct and counsel couples before and during marriage. The priest is given many graces from God, as part of his very priesthood, specifically to enable him to perform the duties of his exalted state of life.

Chapter 2

MARRIAGE TODAY

It would not be far from the truth to state that the institution of marriage is currently undergoing a terrible crisis. At no other time in our nation's history have the problems with marriage been so serious.

In saying this, we may appear to be *negative*, but we have decided that the best way to write on the subject of marriage is to begin negatively. Eventually, we will come around to the *positive* side. Our approach is similar to that of the man who intends to renovate the interior of his house. At first, he must be "negative." He must scrape off the old paint and wallpaper. Then he can begin the real work of renovation and improvement. Similarly, we will spend some time on the negative side of marriage, but only for the purpose of presenting a balanced, positive understanding of the great and glorious Sacrament of Matrimony.

WHY DO WE SAY THAT MARRIAGE IS IN A BAD WAY?

1. Easy Breakup

Statisticians tell us that 50 percent of all marriages which take place in the U.S.A. end up in separation and/or divorce. It is an ever-worsening situation. Some marriage experts even predict that as high as 85 percent of the marriages that are taking place now will eventually break up.

Whatever figures we accept, it is undeniable that there is an appalling amount of discord among married couples—often within our own families and among our friends and co-workers. At a school reunion, it is not unusual to discover that half of our old classmates are divorced. The trend seems to be more and more toward unsuccessful marriages, rather than successful ones.

The *basic* reason for this phenomenon is simple: *An absence of faith* on the part of one or both spouses. In other words, an absence of belief in God's teachings and in God's laws. *The glue that keeps marriages intact is belief in God and the practice of His Holy Religion.*

God is the author of marriage. *He* made the rules governing this sacred institution. Chief among these rules is the fact that marriage is *indissoluble;* that is, it is *unbreakable.* It lasts until the death of one of the partners.

But, there has been a rise of secular humanism, selfishness, loss of faith and lessening of prayer life. In movies, on television and in the secular media, there is generally a harmful message, one that is repeated often—and often in a subtle, predigested manner: "Divorce is commonplace; everyone is doing it; there is nothing morally wrong with it. Do your own thing. You have to be fulfilled! God understands." (In other words, "Seek your own happiness without adhering to Divine Law.")[1]

Through the liberal media, most Americans have become conditioned to accept divorce and are *weak-*

---

1. There is scarcely anything worse for a child than the divorce of his parents. Divorce is an act of selfishness. One's own happiness is selfishly preferred to the child's welfare. All psychiatrists agree that children need primary caretakers, i.e., parents who take care of them on a daily basis.

ened in their understanding that marriage is a divine and indissoluble institution. When disagreements inevitably arise early in their marriages, many couples quickly resort to threats of "walking out." In former days—when marriage was held in greater respect—couples had the same disputes and arguments, but the idea of separation and divorce was foreign to them. It was taken for granted—through religion, culture, and mores—that spouses were married until the death of one of them. Disagreements and problems were usually worked out; or, at least in the case where one partner was incorrigible, the long-suffering spouse would *endure* the problems through counsel and prayer. They would earn Heaven by accepting their crosses on earth.

In many cases the "endurance" period is rewarded by a change in or even a conversion of the "incorrigible" spouse, with a great increase of mutual love and respect enjoyed in later years together. Such a change in her husband occurred in the life of St. Rita of Cascia, but this type of change can happen in all marriages, and is not just a phenomenon in the lives of the Saints. St. Paul confirms this fact when he says: "The unbelieving husband is sanctified by the believing wife, and the unbelieving wife is sanctified by the believing husband." (*1 Cor.* 7:14).

2. Virtual Divorce

The couples that do not actually break up, but are very unhappy together, pose another very serious problem. They are merely "sticking it out" because of the children, or because their parents would be upset. Whereas this problem is not so bad as an *actual* break-up, it is a sign that the marriage is in trouble. What are the reasons for this sad state?

a. Lack of Enthusiasm

We all know of homes in which the couple simply "makes the best of it." If they had it to do all over again, they say, they would *not* have gotten married. They *envy* single people for their freedom and absence of responsibility. People who lack enthusiasm for their own marriages do not *live* for their marriages. Jobs, careers and recreation are more exciting. It is a standard joke in our present society that if a young *man* announces to his co-workers that he has become "engaged," he is ridiculed for taking on a "ball and chain." On the other hand, when a young *woman* announces her engagement, her co-workers energetically congratulate her for landing a husband. But it is a different story for the young man. While there is a certain amount of levity connected with his announcement, the "boys" chide him for taking on a responsibility that he will soon regret.[2]

This lack of enthusiasm toward marriage is symptomatic of the unhappiness and lack of fulfillment that many experience in their own marriages.

b. Separate Interests

While husband and wife may reside under the same roof, separate interests may keep them apart for long periods of time. Of course, there is the obvious and necessary separation which occurs when the breadwinner husband goes off to work while his wife remains at home with the children.

But in our "keep-up-with-the-Joneses" society, there is the all too common phenomenon where the husband works a full-time job, while his wife also holds outside full-time employment. Sometimes their work-

2. Who ever thought up the idea of those horrible stag parties the night before the Sacrament?

hours are on different shifts, so that they hardly see each other.[3]

In addition to his job that takes him away from his home, the husband may participate in some "recreational" activities, such as bowling or membership in a club. Or, whereas the husband may leave the house only infrequently, he may have an inordinate attachment to television or some other activity at home. As a result, there is little time for the couple to do things *together* or to communicate in depth.

Years ago, when our society was largely agricultural, husbands and wives worked together on the farm, ate meals together and, even when out of each other's sight, were never far away from each other. In our present society, because of separate interests, sufficient time is not spent together. *Love* increases as *knowledge* increases. Love in marriage is a quality that does not remain *static,* i.e., motionless. If it does not grow, it diminishes. Love is a function of the will, and the will can only respond to those things *presented by the intellect.* The more a man and woman get to know each other, the greater is their potential to grow in love. It is similar to growth in the love of God, our Creator. The more we know about God, the more we understand His attributes—such as His goodness, mercy, power, wisdom, justice—and the greater becomes our potential to love Him.

c. Lack of Sympathy and Understanding

Most young people *enter* marriage with an incomplete understanding of their spouse, later declaring

---

3. Once a housewife takes employment outside the home, she usually becomes reluctant to leave that employment. The charms of the secular workplace, with its attendant salary, can sometimes make the home seem, by comparison, to be unglamorous and routine.

that they thought the other to be "different." Each originally found in the other an "ideal." Faults were never dwelled upon. Each admired the qualities he or she discovered in the other person, such as how nicely "the intended" treated the other's parents. "When *he* visited my home, he gave respectful attention to my Dad; they talked about topics from baseball to business, and he nodded politely when political questions arose."

"And *she* . . . she was so pretty and feminine! She was enthusiastic and bubbly and made few demands." Just to sit and talk with each other was considered to be a perfect evening.

But an accurate knowledge of each other's faults was missing, or at least minimized in their minds, and often dismissed with comments like, "Of course, we know each other's faults! What do you think we are: immature? But we are in love. We'll work things out!"

Time Marches On: If we could "fast-forward" in real time to perhaps five years later, we may find that this young man and young woman now have many complaints about each other. "He leaves the kitchen sink in a mess . . . and the bathroom, too!"

"She cries or becomes moody when she can't win an argument. She also talks on the phone all day long to her mother and her girlfriends. What the heck do they talk about?"

"Without make-up she scares me!"

"He is so fussy about what he eats. The other day I accidentally broke the yolk on a fried egg, and he wouldn't eat it."

"In the morning she's so grouchy . . . and she looks awful, too!"

"When he gets home from work, he hardly talks to me. And here I am all day with the children, looking forward to his adult company. He is *tired* . . . or so he says. All he wants is a can of beer and his television."

Sounds like a classic situation! After living together for a few years, there tends to be a *lack of sympathy* for the other spouse.

"Yes, *before* the wedding day, we had slight hints as to each other's faults, but *now* they mean so much more. We live together day after day and find it is a headache putting up with those faults and idiosyncrasies!"

One husband remarked to a priest friend of mine: "Father, my wife and I *never* have an argument . . . as long as she doesn't talk to me."

Household Repairs

A great "wall of love" was evident on the wedding day. It was pristine and without flaw. But sometimes a wall begins to show wear and tear, like cracks in the plaster from a house "settling."

So, *repair the cracks,* by pouring in forgiveness, unselfishness and greater understanding, not by resorting to arguments, bitterness and inflexibility. Patch up that wall with virtuous acts, with humor and prayer . . . and with renewed effort to please God and your beloved spouse.

d. Weakening of Home Life

1. *Home has become a "service station."*

In modern America, just as a car pulls into a gas station, fills up on gasoline, has its oil checked and then drives away, so do family members come and go from their homes. The children come home, hurriedly eat supper, do a few little chores and then move on. There is not enough time taken to develop human friendship, not enough togetherness. In God's plan, the home is not merely a place to eat and shower and sleep, like the Y.M.C.A. It is a place to work together, to pray together, to laugh together, to learn together—and indeed, to save your souls together.

2. *A bigger collection of appliances does not necessarily make a happy home.*

The secular world tends to equate a successful home with the number and quality of modern conveniences: Is it not true that at bridal showers and wedding receptions it is usual to see tables overflowing with gifts? During the course of the afternoon, the guests will inspect the tables. Electric toasters, candelabra, linens and blankets—many, many wonderful gifts. Can we not almost hear the guests exclaim: "Look at all these beautiful gifts. Won't they be *happy!*"

There it is! People often equate happiness and marital success with the accumulation of material things.

A young wife faced with the daily chores of kitchen work might complain: "If only I had a dishwasher, I would be absolutely, positively happy!" While the acquisition of a dishwasher, no doubt, would ease some of the burden of the beleaguered housewife, *it will not make her happy!* Many women who have (or had) completely modern kitchens are *divorced.*

We cannot judge a marital union by material possessions. The *norm of success* must always be the *fulfillment of God's will:* the daily living out of the joys and sufferings of life in union with the teachings and example of Our Saviour.

3. *Artificial Entertainment*

Television, of course, is the first thing that comes to mind when we think of artificial entertainment, but there are other forms of artificial recreation as well.

During the engagement period, couples fully enjoy *each other's company.* They are eager to communicate with each other—to *talk* and *talk* and *talk* about their dreams, ideas, fears, failures, hopes. *All subjects*—political, educational, cultural, current events, human nature—make up the conversational spectrum.

After only a few years into marriage, the tendency is to communicate *less.* Instead of exploring each other's intellect and enjoying each other's company, there is a dependence upon entertainment *outside of both.* We can easily imagine a married couple sitting in the living room watching a TV show. Neither party has any input or contribution; both are passive "couch potatoes."

In order for marital love to grow, *interaction* is required. A flowering plant must be given attention in the form of water and sunlight. Some effort is required on the part of the gardener to make the flower grow and bloom. In order for marital love to increase and flourish, there is a need for the *sunlight of conversation.*

e. Prevalence of Adultery

Mental Adultery: When marriage vows are made, man and woman, in effect, promise to be "*one* in mind, *one* in heart, and *one* in affection." Otherwise, they could not very well fulfill their marriage vows. No *thing* and no *person* should take precedence over their mutual love and affection.

Mental unfaithfulness occurs when someone else receives *primary* affection. It could happen if a wife extends more attention to her relatives, or if a husband extends more attention to his friends, or has too much attachment to a career or hobby. When a husband is "always out"—not necessarily in an immoral activity—it means that his affections tend to focus upon subjects other than his wife and family.

Parenthetically, although husbands and wives have

vowed to be *first* in each others' hearts, a wife may become *subtly* guilty of inattention to her husband after the children start to come. She finds it necessary to spend most of her time and energy on the children. Wives and mothers may unconsciously and gradually *drift away from intimacy* with their husbands because they are always busy, that is, occupied and attentive to their babies. A home should not be, *per se,* "child-centered," but more correctly, "God-centered." And this includes the spouses' also remaining attentive to each other and one another's needs.

Physical Adultery: In the secular and atheistic element of human society, adultery has always been a common practice. This is mortally sinful and results in punishment by Almighty God, even in this world!

In our watered-down "Christian" society, adultery is not so socially scandalous as it once was. The liberal media regularly portray infidelity as some kind of romantic adventure—and often attempt to justify, and even *encourage* it. The sin of adultery is euphemistically called "having an affair."

In the civil law, divorce has become simplified and easy to attain. The notoriety of public figures who flaunt their adulterous behavior tends to break down respect for the institution of marriage and the virtue of purity. Scandal and bad example can be found everywhere, often even in the best of families.

A wedding ring placed on the hand of a bride should send out a signal, loud and clear: She belongs exclusively to *one man.* So also the wedding band worn by the groom: He is no longer "fair game." He belongs to *one woman* only.

A respectable married man not only does not commit adultery, but also *does not engage in looks, words* and *actions* which may lead in that direction. On his deathbed, Saint Dominic assured his followers that

he had never fallen into the sin of impurity. He con-
fided that his success was due to the fact that he
"never took part in any dangerous conversations."
That is a good lesson for all of us: *Resist the beginnings!* Many spiritual directors pass that wise maxim
on to their penitents. It is an extremely important
principle in the spiritual life.

Every sinner—from Adam and Eve to every mur-
derer, thief and adulterer since then—has *foolishly
ignored* this principle. Every teenager who has rebelled
against his parents and against God, somewhere along
the line, has refused to "resist the beginnings."

A prudent married person does not bestow any
type of affection on or give more than passing attention to members of the opposite sex which may ultimately lead to fatal consequences. Little by little,
imprudent behavior can weaken one's resolve to
observe faithfully the marriage vows made before
God.

Adultery remains always a mortal sin. It is a direct
violation of the Sixth Commandment. Even if this
sin becomes prevalent in the world, its culpability is
not thereby diminished. Anyone who dies having com-
mitted this sin—and dies unrepentant—will be sub-
jected to eternal punishment in Hell.

f. The Materialism of Modern Marriages

1. Marriage is sometimes considered to be more of
an economic venture than a sacred union. Young people often think of marriage as an opportunity for
them to flourish economically: To take expensive trips,
to eat in the best restaurants and to do many secular things they were not able to do before marrying.

But realistically, marriage is going to provide many
more opportunities for financial *sacrifice* than for the
enjoyment of luxuries. This is especially true where

the couple is willing to accept the children God sends them. The mature Christian viewpoint requires young couples to be *reasonably* prepared for marriage, financially and materially, but at the same time to *trust* in Divine Providence.

When God grants husband and wife the privilege of being parents, they can be sure that, somehow or other, they *will manage.* They may not live as luxuriously as some of their friends. They may not function on the economic level which they would prefer. Nevertheless, married couples should be willing to accept the dispositions of Divine Providence and *gracefully accept* their current, temporary economic conditions as God's Holy Will.

We must remember that the model for the Christian family is the Holy Family. The Holy Family lived quite modestly. They remained in a humble stable for a time and permanently lived in a rather poor area of the world: Palestine and Nazareth. Mary and Joseph had, you might say, a most successful marriage, a most holy marriage, a marriage most pleasing to God. Materialism and financial status were the furthest things from their minds.

2. People tend to adopt the dictum of living *"well,"* instead of living "good." "Good" means that your primary concern is to have your children grow up in the love and fear of God. Living "well" primarily means that you want your children to have all the material things that perhaps you never had. This parental ambition is very often overdone. Of course it is normal and natural for parents to want their children to have the *necessary* things, such as food and clothing and shelter. But to desire one's child to rise on the economic ladder or in the social register, so to speak, can be a very dangerous thing—*if that goal is given priority.* Parents must definitely and clearly establish that their primary obligation toward

their children is to enable them to save their immortal souls. That should be their *top priority.* Everything else pales in comparison to that. *If there is true love for one's children, then salvation should be the number one objective. After all, love is eternal.* We all earnestly desire *not to be separated* from our loved ones. Since life on earth is transient and temporary and since eternity goes on and on without end, we naturally wish to be united *for eternity* with our beloved children. Our children, after all, are the *only* thing we can actually take with us from this life. Therefore, even for selfish reasons, one might say, we should labor unstintingly for the salvation of our children. Why? So that we will all dwell together and irrevocably in the final domicile of Heaven.

g. Conclusion

The chief cause of marital breakup, or unhappiness in marriage, is *selfishness*—which is really a disguised form of *childishness.* Sometimes marriage problems are not truly *marriage* problems. The fault often lies with the *individual,* who puts himself *first* . . . before God, before his spouse and before his children. This selfishness is most evident in the husband who wants to achieve *his own* satisfaction and *his own* happiness first, or in the woman who puts *her own* happiness, *her own* "fulfillment," before that of her husband and her children.

Only God can correctly teach us and demand the sublimation of ourselves and of our individual lives in the interest of that deeper and wider life that we have in common in marriage. *Only God* can instruct us, and only Jesus Christ and His Blessed Mother and St. Joseph can give us the example of how we should work this out in our daily lives. Selfishness can be *converted* to unselfishness, *if* we focus our attention upon *God,* our Creator, and upon the Holy Family and firmly resolve to keep God's laws and follow the example of the Holy Family.

If married couples work toward this beautiful unselfishness in which they think first not of themselves, but rather of God, their spouse and their children, they will not only be sanctified, but will find the greatest degree of happiness that may be allotted to man in this "valley of tears." It is the great irony of life that *unselfishness* leads to a greater degree of happiness than *selfishness*. The secular world views things differently. The more we pursue our own gratification, says the world, the happier we will be. *Just the reverse is true!* The more we seek our own gratification at the expense of others, the unhappier we become and, paradoxically, the less complete and fulfilled as a human being. Good moral principles always win out in the end. Selfish human whims lead to a psychological wrecking ground. Some people hop from one garden to another, trying to find the elusive bird of happiness, while as always, it can be found in one's own backyard, in the presence of God and in following the virtuous behavior displayed by each member of the Holy Family.

Chapter 3

THE POSITIVE SIDE OF MARRIAGE: GOD AND MARRIAGE

AXIOM NO. 1: MARRIAGE BELONGS TO GOD.

This statement sounds true enough to most people, but we are referring here not simply to marriage *in general,* but to *your* marriage.

You may say: *"My* marriage? Well, that is my *own* business." People instinctively want no one on the "outside looking in"—not family, not neighbors, not the priest, not the Church . . . yes, not even God Himself!

Why does *my* marriage belong to God? For *two important reasons:*

We Are All His Creatures.

Through God's creation, we were all made out of nothing. In addition, we were created as human beings in our own unique circumstances, out of millions of possibilities.

Through God's conservation, we are maintained in existence every moment of our lives. Theologians term conservation in existence, *creatio continuata*—"continued creation."

If the Lord withdrew His conserving power from us, *even for one second,* we would lapse into nothingness. We would be "annihilated."

17

Through God's concurrence all our actions need God's sustaining power. We are unable to act, think, do good, or do evil, unless God concurs ontologically, that is, unless He continues to give us our being and thus the ability to function.

Therefore, everything we have and every ability we possess has come from God. *We are completely dependent upon Him!*

NOTE: When rational beings admit this dependence, they are taking the first steps in an act of *worship.* "To worship," according to the dictionary, is to admit one's total dependence on another and consequently to praise that person accordingly. All rational creatures *must* worship God. The First Commandment requires it. It is the basis of life and of religion and must be reaffirmed in good times and in bad.

God Instituted Marriage.

Shortly after the creation of the first man and woman, God united them in the union of marriage (*Genesis* 1-4). Marriage, therefore, is the oldest institution on earth, having been established in the Garden of Eden.

Because God instituted this union, it is sacred for *all* peoples, all races and all religions, not only Christians.

The institution of marriage is not a *human* creation, such as the credit union, the Elks Club or a business partnership. It was not invented by "prehistoric cavemen," by a professor of sociology, or even by a clever female psychologist. No! Marriage was instituted *by our Creator!* The authorship of the institution of marriage belongs to God.

AXIOM NO. 2: GOD LAYS DOWN THE RULES.

Since our Creator instituted marriage, He had the right to make the laws governing this sacred bond.

Therefore, if a couple wishes to marry, they must be willing to keep God's laws regarding the marriage union. To give an example, if an athlete wants to participate in the game of baseball, he must be willing to *abide by the rules* (3 strikes, 3 outs, 4 bases, etc.). If he does not intend to observe these basic rules, then he cannot play the game. Similarly, if the purchaser of an automobile wishes to operate it, he must obey the "rules" of the manufacturer. He must put *gas* in the tank, *oil* in the crankcase, etc. If he refuses to observe these rules and instead pumps ginger ale into the tank, the car will not function. In other words, we are obliged to keep the *rules of life.* If we do not keep the rules of marriage, which were enacted by God, then the marriage will not work.

Now, one of the built-in or inherent aspects of marriage (whether the marriage is good or bad), as long as it is a *valid* and *consummated marriage*—is *indissolubility.* Thus, if John and Mary are married, then they later "divorce" and John "remarries" Sue, he is not married to Sue at all. He is still married to Mary—even if he and Mary both want to be "loosed" from each other. This is what is meant by the *indissolubility of marriage.* In God's eyes, divorce does not count. It does not make a wife into an "ex-wife" or a husband into an "ex-husband." John and Mary are still married until one of them dies—"until death do us part."

Incidentally, an *annulment* (more properly called a "declaration of nullity") granted by the Catholic Church is *not* the dissolving of a marriage. Rather, it is a declaration that the "marriage" was invalid, that is, that the couple were never married in the first place, because of some major defect *at the time of the "marriage."* For example, if one of the parties had intended to be entering only a *temporary* union, no marriage would have taken place, even though the words of the marriage vows were said. (Only a Church tribunal can judge that a particular marriage was invalid and can be declared null.)

The Free Will of Human Beings

Man is not *physically* constrained to keep God's moral laws. Because he has a rational soul, with free will, he can *deliberately disobey*—if he chooses to. Inanimate objects are given no choice: In a metaphysical sense, they *must* obey. Thus, water *must* freeze at 32 degrees above zero.

But man has a *spiritual* soul and *spiritual* obligations. He must give an account to Almighty God *spiritually,* in this life as well as at the Last Judgment.

Breaking God's laws always results in failure in life. For example, to separate from and "divorce" one's validly married spouse is to break God's law. Even if man-made laws recognize divorce, it is *God's* law ultimately that matters in life and in eternity. God's law not only does not *permit* divorce, it does not even *recognize* divorce as a reality.

Man's Weakness

Because of the effects of Original Sin, human beings are frequently *tempted* to disregard God's laws. Our judgment becomes clouded and our resolve tends to weaken. When faced with stresses, temptations and fatigue, humans must turn *to God* for help and strength. Reliance upon the false but often attractive-sounding and on-the-surface philosophies of the secular humanists will only bring misery and eventual damnation.

AXIOM NO. 3: MARRIAGE IS A VOCATION.

From the root meaning of the word "vocation," it is clear that "vocation" means "a calling" (*vocare*— "to call"). We can say that married people are *called* to marriage; they *desire* it above other desires.

Where does the calling or desire come from? A seven-year-old girl dislikes boys. And young boys "hate" girls. For young boys to "like" a girl is to be a "sissy." But as the years go on, boys and girls are drawn together. Where did this "new" idea in their lives come from? Where did the urge come from? The answer is "from God's creative plan."

The choice of a marriage partner will have tremendous spiritual consequences both in this life and in the next. It will have consequences not only for the couple themselves but also for their children, grandchildren, etc. This is why it is so important to choose a serious, believing, practicing Catholic for a spouse. Emotions have an important role to play in this decision, but one must definitely also use one's *head* when considering someone as a potential spouse.

Also, *daily prayer* is of paramount importance in choosing a marriage partner. Through prayer we call upon the mysterious Providence of God. God can and does steer people toward the precise vocation, person, and life's work that He wills for them.

For *most* people, marriage is their calling from God. They will work out their salvation as married persons. They will be saved or damned in large part because of how they dealt with their marriage.

When a young couple are in love with each other and plan to get married, they should not stop at being in love with *each other*. *They should be in love also with the vocation of marriage.* They should be enthusiastic about the primary purpose of marriage, which is to raise up new saints for Heaven. They should have an outlook similar to that of a priest on the day of ordination, or of a nun or brother on the day of profession. They should be saying to themselves: "I am entering upon a great work, a work that will have consequences for all eternity. I will try my best to help my spouse save and sanctify his (her) soul. I want to give new souls to God, and in so doing I plan to save and sanctify my own soul. I *embrace* this life, including the sacrifices it will entail."

There is certainly no room for boredom in marriage with a program as immense and challenging as this.

AXIOM NO. 4: FOR CHRISTIANS, MARRIAGE IS A SACRAMENT.

If both parties are baptized, the sacred union of marriage becomes the *Sacrament of Matrimony*. Like all Sacraments, it is a *source of grace*—as with Baptism, Confirmation, etc. Grace is conferred on the day of the wedding, but additional graces are conferred continually throughout the married life as a direct result of the Sacrament of Matrimony.

We tend to forget this sacramental nature of marriage because of

1. *Civil usurpation*: Until some 300 years ago, there was no such thing as a *civil* marriage. *All* marriages were religious ceremonies. If marriage is merely a civil act, then divorce is merely a civil act.

2. *Secular preparation*: In preparation for the wedding day, a large amount of non-religious activity takes place. Of course, civil requirements, such as a license and blood tests, must be fulfilled. But apart from this, a myriad of details connected with a wedding day are given nervous attention for many months in advance. The reception hall, the menu, the music, the flowers, the gowns, the gifts, and the most diffi-

cult of all, the *invitations*. The problem is not "whom to invite," but rather, "whom *not* to invite." In other words, at what point do we cut off the invitation list? What friends, what business associates, what relatives will be left off? After all, *everyone* cannot be invited.

Much of the focus of the wedding day is on "pleasing our guests," and with this end in mind, much mental and physical energy is expended.

Therefore, the tendency is to forget that a *Sacrament* is to be received: the holy, sacred, unique Sacrament of Matrimony. Jesus Christ should be the most important name on the guest list, the principal member of the bridal party.

For Our Greater Understanding

Compare Marriage as a Sacrament to other Sacraments.

1. *First Holy Communion Day.* This is the first time that the Body and Blood of Jesus Christ will be received into one's own person.

Yes, there *is* some secular preparation, such as a white dress, a new suit and perhaps a party to follow. But overwhelming attention is always given to the spiritual and educational preparation for this Sacrament. The "spiritual" truly takes precedence over the "secular."

2. *Holy Orders.* A young man steps forward in the cathedral sanctuary to receive the Sacrament of Holy Orders. He receives the powers of the priesthood from the consecrating hands of the bishop.

Of course, considerable attention has been given to the dinner and reception which follows and to the well-wishing of his friends. But, at no time does anyone forget or cast into the background the fact that a momentous Sacrament is being conferred. Semi-

nary training in theology, the development of prayer
habits and the practice of virtue, all led up to this
day. A great Sacrament which confers enormous graces
is being received. *Deo Gratias!*

Live up to the Graces of the Sacrament.

When we die and face the Judgment, as *we all
must,* we shall certainly have to answer for our sins
of neglect. Please God that we will be able to say to
the Divine Judge that we have been faithful to our
vocation, whichever vocation God has called us to.

The Purpose of Marriage

When God made marriage, as indeed He did, He
acted for a *good reason.* Our Creator, unlike frail
human beings, does not do things out of poor judgment, anger or nervousness. He always acts from a
fountain of Infinite Wisdom.

AXIOM NO. 5: CHILDREN ARE THE PRIMARY PURPOSE OF MARRIAGE.

The primary purpose of marriage is "to procreate"
and raise children—that is, to co-operate with God
in the creation and rearing of new human beings.

1. Every child is made in the image and likeness
of God. Each is a "potential adorer" of God and a can-
didate for everlasting happiness in Heaven. Every person has this same destiny. Therefore, every child must
be considered to be beautiful and wanted. This is true
even if a child has a physical or mental handicap. In
fact, a child with a handicap may have a greater
chance of achieving his eternal destiny than does a
"perfect" child.

Compared to all of the products of human inge-
nuity, a child is by far to be treasured the most. Sup-

pose a mother took her baby and stood next to the
Great Pyramid of Egypt or the Empire State Building in New York City and asked herself, "Which is
greater, my baby or this great edifice?" The question
would answer itself: "Some day this building will cease
to exist, but my baby has an *immortal soul*: He will
live forever in eternity. My child is more precious
than any transient work of man."

2. Since the begetting and rearing of children con-
stitutes the primary end or purpose of marriage, marriage must be looked upon as an *unselfish* venture.
The welfare of *others* comes *before personal* aggran-
dizement. This *altruism* is similar to the purpose of
the priesthood. A young man does not enter into a
priestly vocation primarily for *personal* happiness,
but rather for the *good of souls*. Likewise, marriage
is not primarily for personal happiness. It was instituted principally for the purpose of producing can-
didates for Heaven.

An engaged man and woman look forward to shar-
ing a home with someone they love, to a lifetime of
security, romance and companionship. This is all well
and good! But they should remember that, first of all,
they must open up their hearts to God's creative power
and be willing to live for *others* in an unselfish way.[4]

3. *The Dignity of Parents.* The secular world frowns
upon a large family. Non-believers are often critical
of parents who have procreated many children. This
is due to the fact that the secular world thinks only
of itself and *its* happiness. It has a self-centered, "get-
all-the-gusto-you-can" philosophy, without any regard

---

4. We once asked a young man at whose wedding we had offi-
ciated ten years previously: "What is the most difficult aspect
of marriage?" He pondered for a moment, then said tri-
umphantly, "The most difficult thing? It is being thoughtful
all the time."

for the Kingship of God.

One thing is certain, however: *Parenthood is an obligation* of marriage (unless a couple is unable to have children). It is also a wonderful privilege, because

a. *Parents are co-creators.* New human beings are God's greatest work, and parents have the honor of being God's chosen instruments in producing and raising them. To quote from the marriage ritual: "You are called to work with God in the greatest work of creation—the continuation of the human race."

b. *Children are a lasting achievement.* Almost everything else we humans produce is transient, trivial and cheap. As we stated before, this is not true of the baby whose mother took it and stood next to the Empire State Building, looked up at that massive structure of steel and cement, and then, letting her gaze come down into the face of her infant, asked a simple question: "Which is greater—this great 102-story building or my little baby?"

There is no contest! Someday the Empire State Building will be gone; whereas, the child has an immortal soul. He has the ability to love God forever and ever—longer than all of the world's buildings will ever last and longer than a thousand thousand generations.

Mutual Love and Help

Mutual love and help is the *secondary* purpose for marriage in God's plan, but a very, very important one, nevertheless!

Couples entering marriage often have a mistaken idea of *love.* They confuse infatuation or passion with love. They often also confuse "like" with "love."

1. To *"like"* is to *receive* pleasure or enjoyment.

2. To *"love"* is *to give,* that is, to do what is good for the beloved. To understand the meaning of love, look at the word "benevolence." This word contains

the elements of genuine love.

Taken from the Latin *bene* ("well") and *volens* ("wish"), "benevolence" thus means "to wish well" or what is "good" for someone else. Consequently,

a. If I love my children, I wish *their* good.

b. If I love my husband or his parents, I want what is good for *them.*

c. If I love God, I want what is good *for God.*

NOTE: In all these loves, there is not necessarily an emotional uplift. The motive for love lies in the *will,* that is, in the desire and act of our spiritual faculty. We may call love a *"determination"* to do what is good for another. And there are many marvelous examples of this determination to be found in the lives of the Saints, who loved God above all things. Examples also can be found in the lives of many parents who continually sought what was good for their children and proved it by their many sacrifices. That was true love—*in action,* not merely in theory.

Addendum

Holy Scripture tells us: "Love your enemies." (*Matt.* 5:44). Yes, we are to love even our *enemies*! How can we do this? Simply by applying the principle of "benevolence." To love one's enemy means to wish what is *good* for him, that is, that he be converted, and perhaps punished, or even removed from society. We want what is *best* for *him.* (It is not necessarily "good" or charitable to make excuses for evildoers.)

Love of Man and Woman

Each partner in the marriage should be the recipient of sincere and effective desires by the other for his or her spiritual, emotional and physical good. One's individual likes or dislikes should be subordinated to the good of the beloved.

For example, on a Sunday afternoon, the husband might like to watch a football game. The wife, whom he loves, would prefer to visit her relatives. The husband makes an act of love by doing what is pleasing to his beloved—willingly putting aside his own personal likes for *her* sake. It is a sacrifice—an unselfish Christian act done generously. The lives of the Saints are filled with such acts. There is certainly an element of heroism in such acts, especially if they are practiced continually. They may or may not be appreciated by one's spouse, but they will be amply rewarded by God, either in this life or the next, or both.

In marriage, the secret of happiness lies in the willingness to think of the *other* person.

Conversely, the "public-enemy-number-one" of love is *selfishness*. "*Me* first, and *you* second" spells an unhappy marriage. *Mutual love* in marriage means *mutual help*.

Mutual Love

1. Husband and wife *need* each other. Human hearts were made for love, and they are not complete unless they give love and receive love in return. One need merely look at the loving hearts of the Holy Family: the Blessed Mother, Saint Joseph and our divine Saviour, Jesus Christ. They showed the world the need for love, as well as the correct way to practice it.

2. Man and woman are made by God in such a psychological and physical mode that they are made to complement each other. In marriage, one is not complete without the other.

3. By loving each other, husband and wife help each other to keep the Faith and to practice virtue, and they support one another on the road to eternal salvation. Human beings benefit greatly by good exam-

ple, and this is never more evident than in a good marriage. The prayerfulness and trust in Divine Providence of the wife give strength to the husband. And at other times, the situation is reversed. In this way, arm in arm, they walk through life supporting, helping and encouraging each other.

Education of Offspring

Education of Children is also part of God's plan:

1. Parental duty does not stop with procreation, but rather *increases* dramatically as a result of it. Infants are absolutely helpless and need parents for many years.

2. Education here is taken in the *wider sense* of forming the *whole* person: physically, socially, intellectually and spiritually.

The father and mother are the *first teachers*. Children tend to *imitate* their parents, although they very soon come to use their own intellect and have their own character. The education process, begun at home, should train children's intellects and wills and form them after the inexhaustible teaching and example of our Saviour, Jesus Christ.

Neither the state, the school system, nor even the Church itself can usurp the primary responsibility of parents to educate their own children. To them alone belongs the right and duty to lead their children to eternal salvation. In this, the *home is first;* all else remains supplementary.

Chapter 4

TOGETHERNESS, or
THE UNION OF MIND AND HEART
(Differences between Male and Female)

STATE OF THE QUESTION

The *physical* union is beautiful and essential. But more importantly, a union of *heart and mind* is required for a happy marriage.

a. Holy wedlock is a union of two rational beings. Since a human being is a rational creature, made by God with body *and* soul, a union of bodies alone is not sufficient for husbands and wives. Consider, for example, the so-called Hollywood marriages. These liaisons are based primarily on physical attraction and rarely last for more than a few years.

Practicing Catholics crave a union of *persons,* that is, of heart and soul. This craving exists on both the natural and supernatural levels. It is a dictum of spiritual direction that "the supernatural builds on the natural."

The union between two normal human beings is a *"dynamic"* one, that is, it is a loving, *changing* relationship. It is unlike the union of inanimate objects, such as a welded joint, which remains fixed and unchanged.

A union of minds and hearts can never be taken for granted. Since humans grow, learn, experience, improve, get new ideas, develop new tastes . . . in short, since we change from year to year, and sometimes even from week to week or day to day, there must be frequent adjustment between two married people. Maintaining the serene, uncomplicated harmony typical of the early years of a marriage requires a willingness to "flex" as time goes on.

b. Married lives are not *"one"* until the man and woman have achieved a certain degree of unity, both mentally and emotionally. Most married couples are more or less compatible, but none is 100 percent so. They may be 80 percent or 90 percent compatible, which is good! But the remaining 20 percent or 10 percent needs attention, guidance and understanding.

COMMON "NORMAL" COMPLAINTS

Typical signs of *normal* incompatibility are such common complaints as:

1. "My husband doesn't understand me."

2. "I cannot figure my wife out. She acts differently than I would."

3. *He:* "What's the matter, Hon?"

   She: "You know what's the matter!"

   He: "No, I really don't. Please tell me."

   She: "You do know. Don't put on an act!"

   He: "No, I honestly don't know."

   She: "Stop pretending that you don't know!"

   He: "For crying out loud! I have no idea what's the matter!" Then shouting and anger.

NOTE: These types of complaints may surface after one year of marriage, or 30 days. The passage of time does not eliminate personality traits, gender differences, free will or the tendency to change.

Nevertheless, we all have a personal obligation to grow spiritually, to work towards the elimination of our faults and to increase in virtue in order to be a good, interesting person to live with.

Too Many Nagging Wives

Often there is a lack of understanding and a lack of patience on the part of the wife.

Definition of Nagging: "To try, constantly and overtly, to change what a person *will not* or *cannot* change." For example: a husband's way of walking, his slowness to make household repairs, his disorganization, his unwillingness to ask directions when driving, or his inability to get promotions in the workplace.

Indeed, a wife should encourage her husband to improve in those areas in which he needs improvement. But it must be done with prayer, good example and the subtle use of that feminine influence, which is one of God's gifts to every woman.

Too Many Hard-Headed Husbands

Many men are overly conscious of *their* rights and are consequently too demanding. After being "Boss" in his place of business—and sometimes influenced by a false, secular conception of masculinity—a man may tend to be unbending. While he must not forget that he is constituted by God to be "head" of the household, he must remember that authority has limits. He must never act in a tyrannical or unreasonable manner. His wife should be a true *"partner"* in the sacred work of keeping a home and raising a family.

When God fashioned Eve, the first woman, He constituted her as a "helpmate," not a servant or slave. (Cf. *Genesis* 2:18).

Senseless Quarrels Over . . .

a. *Children*: Offspring should bring mother and father closer together, not drive them farther apart.

Any disagreements over discipline, freedoms, style of clothing, etc., should be "talked over" and settled out of earshot of the children.

b. *Money*: Often one spouse is a "spender"; whereas, the other one is a "saver." A middle ground is probably the best solution.

c. *Pride*: No one likes to lose an argument or admit that the other person is right and "I am wrong." But why not? Each spouse should seek truth and wisdom, not victories.

d. *Relatives and Friends*: Each spouse must keep in mind that the other spouse comes *first*—in both time and affection—before relatives and friends. To maintain this primacy of affections, it will take vigilance and unselfishness. It must be worked at!

Lack of Confidence

Each spouse must respect the other's judgment, as well as his or her sincerity and unselfishness. Loyalty and love should be as natural and consistent as the morning sunrise.

NOTE: During the time of courtship and the beginning of married life, all these considerations seem insignificant; indeed, one might say, unnecessary. At that time in the marriage, after all, the couple's attitude is, "We love each other," and "Love will conquer all."

Normal Problems

Q. Why are there problems?

A. Because engaged couples get to know each other *only to a limited degree.*

Q. Why?

A. *Because of youth.*

To marry young in life, generally speaking, is God's will for most who marry. If couples knew *too* much about the vicissitudes of life and the inconsistency of human nature, perhaps they might be overcautious and cynical and never marry. Marriages would become fewer and fewer.

Youth has *strength,* and youth has *weakness.* Its strength lies in its energy, health, eagerness—all of which are conducive to procreation and parenthood. Its weakness consists in its lack of experience, and often in its lack of judgment.

One should not worry, however. Through God's grace, bestowed through the Sacrament of Matrimony, through daily prayer, through quiet fidelity to duty, there is every opportunity for growth in maturity and spirituality.[5] The perfect model is the youthful Jesus Christ, who "advanced in wisdom, and age, and grace with God and men." (*Luke* 2:52).

Q. Are there other reasons?

A. Yes. *Because of infatuation,* emotional attraction tends to blind us to each other's faults and differences. And even when these shortcomings are known, infatuation often inclines us to gloss over the far-reaching consequences of these faults and differences. *Following is a typical refrain:* "I know he has faults, and I know there are many things we do not agree about, but we *love* each other. We can work things out. He will change for me, because he loves me."

---

5. If a potential spouse is a heavy drinker, or uses drugs, one should not realistically expect him (or her) to reform in marriage. Although spouses often do and really should change for the better in a happy marriage—under the beneficent influence of love and a willingness to share—still, marriage is definitely *not* a reform school and should not be counted on to be such. A more realistic approach before marriage would be to say to oneself about the prospective spouse, "Show me what you have done, and I'll show you what you will do." Or, "Show me what you have been, and I will show you what you will be."

Q. Any other reasons?

A. One more: *The eagerness to marry.*

Single girls see young mothers with their babies. How much they admire those mothers and wish they could imitate them. And besides, if she does not get married *now,* maybe she will end up an "old maid." How much she envies her girl friends who have found a husband and started a home!

Single men, too, are anxious to have sons and daughters, and a good wife to fulfill their heart's desires. Young men also dream dreams: of a son playing little league baseball; a sweet daughter in her party dress, an all-American Catholic home!

Conclusion: Both youth and infatuation are part of God's plan. If a man were older and wiser, perhaps fear of the unknown or his perceived inability to change would prevent him from ever getting married.

If a woman were not infatuated, she might see *too many* faults in her young man and run away from the marriage prospect.

Yes! Thank God for youth and infatuation! They give human beings a "running start" and serve as an antidote to a world weary with cynicism.

But after the passage of time in the marriage, couples become gradually aware, through experience, of the differences that they had previously overlooked. Before marriage, it was mostly *theory*. After entering the marriage state, this knowledge takes on day-to-day practical realizations.

Are these differences between men and women to be classified as "faults," or merely "differences" which emanate from gender or personality?

James Thurber, a popular humorist for *The New Yorker Magazine* in the 1930's and 1940's, made a name for himself by his articles and sketches. His theme was "The Battle of the Sexes." The premise was simple: Point out the differences between the way males and females feel, reason and communicate. Then, find humor in the perplexity each experiences as a consequence of these differences. Thurber tickled the funny bone of men and women across America.

Factors Based on Inherent Differences between the Male Sex and the Female Sex

The opposite sex attracts, *but paradoxically,* it also repels. For example, a woman is attracted to a man as an individual, but not necessarily to the symptoms of *masculinity.* She may hate cigar smoke, football games, prize fights, mustaches and beer drinking, but she loves *this* man, who enjoys all of the above!

A man probably dislikes hair curlers, "girl talk" and lipstick, but he loves *this* woman!

A man or woman wants to be loved as a *person,* but also as a person created by God *male* or *female.*

Premise: Men and women are inherently different.

All one has to do to prove this is to scrutinize a brother and a sister from the same home. They have the same parents and the same influences, yet brother and sister are drastically different in not only physical development and bodily strength, but also in inclinations, recreations and interests. The differences become more obvious when the brother and sister grow out of infancy. But even as toddlers, the differences begin to surface. Little boys usually like to "rough-house" with their fathers, play with the dog, climb trees and capture garden lizards. They are not attentive to their personal appearance—traditionally attested by a shirt-tail hanging out and an unruly mop of hair.

From an early age, girls are conscious of their hair style and their attire and would rather have a coloring book than a book about monsters or sports heroes. No football for them! They would rather play house, help Mom in the kitchen or occupy themselves in girls' recreations.

Differences in Man and Woman

Different in Their Vocations

A. *Man is made to "rule," whether in the family, the state or the Church.* This vocation comes from God, but *in order to be exercised properly, God must rule him!* And, he must also know how to *rule himself*! All genuine authority has the Creator as its source. Man must simply carry out, as a human instrument, the designs of God.

God is called "Father," as head of the universe.

A priest is called "Father," as head of the community.

A husband is called "Father," as head of the household.

The man is created to rule, but obviously one could cite many cases in which a man abused this vocation by excessive and near totalitarian use of power. (Feminists are quick to point this out.) But what is far more common are cases in which the man sins by *neglect*. He does not exercise sufficiently strong or consistent leadership.

The secret of responsible masculine authority lies in the example and teaching of our Saviour, Jesus Christ. As Christ the King must rule the society of mankind, so also must men assume leadership in the family.[6]

---

6. Men and women, in one sense, are not equal. There is a hierarchy of authority, as is clear from the Epistle of St. Paul to the Ephesians (Chapter 5). Man is spiritually responsible for his wife and his whole household.

B. *Woman is made to be the heart of the home (while man is constituted its head).* She is created by God, both physically and spiritually, to be a *mother.* Endowed with the wonderful gifts needed to exercise motherhood, she fits into her vocation quite naturally. If, in fact, she is unable to bear children, her motherly talents can be applied to a whole panorama of activity: office work, parish societies, caring for the aged and the sick, and good causes of every kind.

NOTE: The Women's Liberation Movement does a woman no favor by asking her to suppress these marvelous motherly attributes.

This feminine capability also performs an additional service. Sometimes a husband is unwilling or unable to assume proper leadership in the home. In these cases, the wife receives the grace to wear two hats, so to speak—but with difficulty! Yes, history is replete with stories of heroic women, from Joan of Arc and Isabella of Spain, to the housewife of the American pioneer days and the many mothers whose husbands have separated from or divorced them. God has given woman a practical adaptability to meet seemingly every necessity—including leadership, *if she has to.* But she instinctively and naturally defers to the man for this role when she can. And she has a right to expect him to carry the burden of leadership in the home.

Qualities of Heart

By nature a woman is "altruistic" (from the Latin: *altera*—"others"). She tends to think of *others.* A man tends to be egocentric (from the Latin: *ego*—"I"), but not necessarily in a non-virtuous way.

A woman's nature is to give, to be altruistic, to do for others. Her altruism is extended to her children, parents and friends. She quite naturally *wants* to remember birthdays and anniversaries. She likes to do favors and make people happy. The wife buys greeting cards and little gifts. She keeps up correspondence with cousins, aunts and uncles. She makes it a point to see that the children visit Grandma, and she delights in bringing a treat to that widowed aunt in the nursing home.

If a woman cannot "give" at home, she tends to join organizations and auxiliaries, so that she can fulfill these God-given instincts elsewhere.

A *man* tends to take this altruism for granted. He would do himself and his wife a great favor if he would imitate some of the charity and thoughtfulness of his wife.

Intellectual Differences

Man's reasoning process tends to be detached, speculative and universal. He loves to talk politics and feels at home with mathematics. He prides himself in being *logical*.

Woman's reasoning process tends to be warm, colorful, spontaneous and detailed.

Man proceeds step by step from established premises: It takes him longer to reach his conclusions.

Woman has stronger *intuitive* reasoning: She sees all the details at once and comes to a conclusion here and now.

Man tends to be *theoretical*.

Woman tends to be *utterly pragmatic*. She wants practical solutions, not theories. For example, if a classroom question came up: "Could God make a rock that He could not move?"—a *boy* might ponder the inscrutable balance between God's omnipotence and His laws of nature, and then take a guess. A *girl*, on the other hand, would probably respond immediately: "Why would God want to do *that*?"

A woman's practicality and her intuitive knowledge are God-given strengths that prepare her for motherhood. A man would be a mental wreck if he had to make the endless decisions required in the day-by-day rearing of infants. Yet a mother can cut through the maze of logic and make prudent decisions for her babies as easily as taking a drink of water.

A special note: A woman has the knack of arriving at the right answers by way of seemingly insufficient reasons.

For example: A salesman may come to the door selling vacuum cleaners. Even though the wife may need a vacuum cleaner, she may immediately reject the sales pitch. Why? Because the salesman had a button out of place, or a "funny look" in his eye.

There are many, many husbands who have their wives to thank for helping them choose or reject a new business or political associate. Hubby may bring home for dinner a newly found friend who has made an excellent first impression upon him.

After a few hours of pleasant conversation and polite compliments, the newcomer departs. The wife will then caution her husband that "something is not quite right" and urge him *not* to pursue this new friendship.

Usually the wife proves to be correct. In our experience, men have often informed us that their wife's intuition has saved them from egregious errors of judgment.

Adaptability

Man usually *plans*—and acts on those plans.

Woman acts on *events*—and adapts herself as events change. She has the knack of adapting and changing on her way to a specific goal. A man must understand this and not complain that his wife is always "changing her mind."

Men are often mystified as to why a woman changes her mind so often. They forget that events and people change. The woman adapts (changes) to fit the events.

Although this changeableness can be a weakness, more often it is a *strength* in a woman. Adaptability is a wonderful gift. It is bestowed by Almighty God, because woman is created to do things for others.

For example: Many a woman has cared for an invalid mother for months and years, giving up her own established routine in order to adapt to a crisis as it has come up. A man would probably be beside himself in the same situation.

Greater Responsibility to Change

Woman's adaptability enables her to "change" to accommodate her husband more easily than for her husband to change for her.

For example: A farmer marries a city girl. It is easier for the girl to adapt to a farmer's life than for the farmer to adapt to urban life.

If one partner must change lifestyles in marriage, the burden should fall upon the wife—since she has been endowed with this God-given attribute of easy adaptability.

Another example: A husband's job location changes. He is transferred out of state. The wife is marvelously able to make all the necessary adjustments—with the children's schooling, with the budget, with the new environment. She is able to adapt to the new cir- · cumstances.

The death of a spouse: Woman's gift of adaptability becomes especially evident in times of personal sorrow.

When a wife dies, the sorrowing husband often remains lost and confused. But when a husband predeceases the wife, the widow usually adapts much more easily, once the financial matters are taken care of.

Judgment

Man tends to be slow and logical.

Woman tends to be rapid and spontaneous. Her first reaction to things must often be modified.

Conclusion: Each spouse has an obligation.

1. The husband must tactfully correct the wife's judgment now and then, being careful to avoid harsh criticism of *her*.

2. The wife must accept the husband's slowness and not be harshly critical of him because of his lack of spontaneity.

Example: A young 10-year-old son brings home a newly found companion, "a new kid in the neighborhood." When he introduces the boy to his *father*, Dad reels off a series of questions: Where do you live? Do you get good marks in school? Where do you attend Church? Where does your father work? Do you like sports?

Then Dad, based upon the collected data, makes a judgment: "I *like* your new friend."

Later on that day, the son introduces the "new kid on the block" to his *mother*. After *one* glance, without any investigative questioning, immediately Mom proclaims: "I don't like him." (Sometimes she says this *aloud*. Sorry, kids!)

Guess what? Mom is usually right, even though her judgment was intuitive and instantaneous. Why? Because she notices some disturbing detail—perhaps a smirk or manner of dress or hairstyle. This seemingly minor detail actually *spoke volumes* to her!

The way Mom thinks and the way a seasoned personnel director thinks is very similar. Little telltale signs will often disqualify a job applicant to an experienced interviewer.

Example: A man very active in politics told me a story that illustrates this point. Many times he would meet people on the campaign trail who seemed to be genuinely interested in his cause.

Quite often, he would invite such a person to his home for dinner and conversation. After an evening of cordiality, the guest would make his goodbyes and go home. My politician friend would then go back into the living room, relax for a few minutes, and say to his wife:

"Honey, how did you like him?" And his wife would reply:

"I didn't like him."

"Why?"

"I didn't like his looks."

The moral of the story: My politician friend told me that his wife's judgment proved to be extremely accurate. She saved him from getting involved with several undesirable characters.

Imagination

Recall Rodin's statue of "The Thinker." Yes, it is a *male* figure, and it fairly accurately portrays the masculine psyche.

Man is full of *ideas* and *abstractions,* and he is sometimes quite speculative and dull. The *exceptions* are men who are artistically gifted.

Woman: Her thoughts are more lively, although she tends to exaggerate trifles. She can see beyond the immediate circumstances and visualize potential opportunities or pitfalls.

These gender-based differences complement each other and prove helpful to couples when they have to make domestic decisions.

Example: A married couple goes house-hunting. The real estate agent opens the door of a house that is for sale. Husband and wife enter together. The husband examines the floors, walls and windowpanes for durability. Then he goes into the cellar to check the heating unit, the plumbing, the electrical systems, the construction.

What is his wife doing? In *her* mind, she already pictures the right kind of curtains or drapes on the windows. She visualizes the best arrangement for the living room furniture. She is able to imagine the decoration potential of the dining room and the kitchen.

Conclusion: If the marriage were all "masculine," the couple might choose a strong, functional house, but it well might be "cold" and uninviting.

If the marriage were all "feminine," the new house might be beautiful to look at, but structurally weak and functionally deficient.

Together, with both male and female input, the blend is just right: a *strong* house and a *beautiful* home.

The wisdom of God is very evident in having created these differences. Our Creator gives men special strengths, and He gives women special strengths. These qualities combine for the maximum benefit of the family and society. "Male and female He created them." (*Gen.* 1:27). *Deo Gratias!*

Communication—The Use of Language

According to an old adage: "A man says what he means; a woman has to be interpreted."

Man communicates more *directly* and bluntly. He attempts to state facts. He means what he says. He likes to talk about *things.*

Woman communicates *indirectly.* She often talks

"around" a subject. She likes to talk about *people*.

A man must learn to understand what his wife is saying to him. Also, he must understand that his wife, by nature, is interested in what he did all day, where he went, where he had lunch, to whom he spoke, what he said, how he said it, etc.

A man may consider these details insignificant, but his wife, who has been home all day with the children, is hungry for details of the outside world.

In the same vein, we might add that women are interested in *specific* explanations.

Example 1: A husband is late for dinner: It is his own fault. Yet all the way home, he tries to invent some excuse to lessen his culpability. But when he finally gets home and walks in the door, he says simply, "Honey, I'm late and I'm sorry."

Example 2: A wife is late getting home to prepare dinner: She was delayed through her own fault. But when she comes in the door, she tends to talk around various subjects. Sometimes she puts on an act, or plays the role of a blameless maiden. She tends to use verbal footwork, rather than give a direct, brief apology.

Conclusion: Men usually want only a succinct statement of facts.

Women desire a more lengthy explanation.

Ergo: Each spouse should endeavor to provide *for* the other what he or she desires. Be thoughtful and forgiving toward one another. It is the Golden Rule.

Example 3: Indirect communication:

Husband—(It is a Sunday afternoon.) "Honey, would you like to take a ride somewhere?"

Wife—"Yes. That would be nice."

Husband—(Getting into the car.) "Where would you like to go?"

Wife—"Oh, I don't know."

Husband—"It doesn't matter?"

Wife—"No, really, it doesn't (. . . pause). Why don't we take a ride up on Northfield Ave?"

Husband—"Aha! Just what I thought. You want to visit *your Mother.*"

Emotions

Man leads with the *intellect.*

Woman leads with her *emotions.*

NOTE: These are "general" tendencies, but not *absolute* rules in *every* case. Sometimes, for example, a man will get foolishly involved in an unwise situation because he lets emotion overpower his right reason. A woman, too, can let emotion lead her astray.

What are emotions? They might be described as "pre-conceptual volitional reactions." What does *that* mean? In other words, emotions are *the reactions of our wills* ("I *like* this!" or, "I *don't* like that!") *before* we have even formed an abstract idea or concept in our minds. Emotions might be called the first and most fundamental reactions we have to our intuitive knowledge of things. In themselves, emotions are good. They are a built-in reaction to the most fundamental type of knowledge we have. God created us to react this way. Therefore, emotions are part of what we are. Unfortunately, they have a bad reputation. Some people look upon emotion as a sign of weakness, or as a sign of sinfulness. One has only to look upon the face of our Saviour—who mourned over Jerusalem, who wept at the death of Lazarus, who sweat blood in Gethsemane, who strongly condemned hypocrites, who angrily cast out money-changers from the Temple—to realize that Our Lord did not avoid emotion.

In actuality, emotions are the lubricants for the machinery of reason and will. They put conviction into action and can stir us on to great things.

For example: Madam Curie would not have spent

long, arduous hours in her discovery of radium had she not become "emotional" over the number of deaths from cancer. She had a strong reaction to these deaths. *Great leaders* would not rise up to fight for justice, or to combat immorality, unless stirred by emotional surges of patriotism or altruism. *Great Saints,* such as St. Francis Xavier, St. Isaac Jogues, St. Anthony of Padua, were imbued with love of God and of souls. Their love overflowed into their emotions and spurred them on to great missionary efforts.

Loving mothers have spent long dedicated nights at a child's sickbed because these mothers were *emotionally attached* to their offspring.

On the negative side, emotions can "lubricate" bad behavior, such as impatience, envy, over-possessiveness, selfishness, immoral inclinations. If free rein is given to emotions, it can make life difficult for others and dangerous for oneself.

Emotions should be *reasoned* and *willed,* like a rider who controls the horse under the saddle. In marriage the "horses" of emotions should always be kept under control. When emotions are under the control of reason, they become powerful inducements toward goodness, kindness, fidelity to duty, preservation of the family and the spirit of sacrifice.

It is often common for a person to possess one single unreasonable emotion. Husband and wife should know each other's sensitive areas, that is, those things which trigger an unreasonable emotional response. They should stay away from these areas unless some very important *principle* is involved!

Furthermore, it is a good idea to speak about each other's unreasonableness from time to time. This should be done during some quiet, affectionate moment together. But it should not be done *too* often. Note well the following word of caution: "New Agers" greatly overdo the focus on personal sensitivity. It leads to excessive attention to oneself, which is self-centeredness.[6]

---

6. Modernist priests have ruined countless young people by their "How-do-you-feel?" sessions. Typically, New Age clergy place *feelings* above *performance.*

Chapter 5

THE PHYSICAL UNION

INTRODUCTION

The ideal in marriage is "oneness." The closer a husband and wife can become, the more closely they approach this ideal. Marriage is a "union"—a union of two people who are irrevocably linked by God Himself. In the Gospel according to St. Matthew, Jesus Christ affirmed: *"What therefore God hath joined together, let no man put asunder."* (*Matt.* 19:6).

A Lofty Comparison

St. Paul the Apostle went so far as to compare the union of husband and wife to the union of Christ and His Church. The following conclusions may be drawn from his Epistle to the Ephesians (5:22-33):

1. Just as Christ *protects* and fights for His Church, so also a husband must *protect* his spouse, and indeed his marriage.

2. Just as Christ is *faithful* to His Church and will never abandon it, so also the husband and wife must be faithful to each other.

3. Speaking of His Church, Christ proclaimed: "Behold I am with you all days, even to the consummation of the world." (*Matt.* 28:20). (Latin: *usque ad consummationem saeculi*—"even unto the consummation of the ages.") So also husband and wife must remain together until the end of their lives on earth.

4. Just as Jesus is *vigilant* over His Church, so also husbands and wives should be watchful so that imperfections, problems and even enemies will not threaten their marriage.

Mature Love

In holy wedlock, couples should strive to attain the kind of love that *mature* people practice. *Initial infatuation* usually does not endure for very long into the married life. Since it is based on the emotions, infatuation tends to be only surface-deep and transient, dependent to a large extent upon one's moods.

Mature love is that which is *consistent* on every level and in every condition. Not grandiose or highly charged, it is the deep faithfulness of *respect* and *service*. It does not have to be spectacular in the eyes of the world, but always it must be persevering.

Consider the love between fathers and their sons: it is a deep, abiding love, yet it is not necessarily demonstrative. What really matters is loyalty, respect and affection that unfailingly endures year after year.

Mature love in marriage must include similar qualities. It should be present in times of anger or displeasure, as well as in times of joy. It should be present when the other person wants to be "alone for a while," when he or she is tired, or there are money problems, when the wife has not put on her makeup, when the husband is grimy from working in the yard or grouchy from problems at work.

In short, mutual love should be mature and unconditional.

Jesus Christ loves us human beings in this manner. He loves us even when we are grimy and sinful and imperfect. Of course, we must also be aware of Divine Justice. Should we unfortunately die with mortal sin on our souls, we have God's word that we will be lost forever in Hell. Divine perfection—God's justice, mercy, omniscience—all work in an inscrutable harmony.

Nevertheless, God possesses an infinite, unconditional love for all mankind. Husbands and wives should pattern their love for each other upon that love which God possesses for His imperfect children.

The Three Levels of Union

In marriage there should be three levels of union between the husband and wife:

1. *Physical Union*—the intimate coalition of *bodies.*

2. *Union of Minds*—the agreement on intellectual matters, artistic tastes, political persuasions, recreations, budgeting, degree of orderliness in the home, etc.

3. *Spiritual Union*—the agreement on the God-given *purpose of life,* the need for Christ and His Church, the Church's moral and doctrinal precepts in the marriage and the need for supernatural grace.

Of the three unions, the physical is usually the easiest to achieve. The mental is generally more difficult. And the spiritual—which should be a "given" coming into the marriage where both spouses are Catholic—can often take even more effort and sacrifice, especially if one party in the marriage is not Catholic or is a poorly instructed Catholic.

In this chapter we shall focus on the *physical union.*

At the outset, let us say that any discussion of the physical (or carnal) is usually more attention-getting than other subjects. A certain human curiosity is inevitable. But, let us make it clear that our credentials do not enable us to delineate intimate details or clinical facts. Rather, our apostolate is to present rules, guidelines and moral precepts—all based on the teachings of Holy Mother Church and sound psychological principles.

How Important Is the Physical Union?

The bodily consummation of a marital union is *fundamental* to making the union a consummated marriage. Its action complements and seals the words of the marriage vows. Without it, the marriage bond and "contract" has not been completed.

Q.—How fundamental is it?

A.—If a couple discovered that one partner is incapable of the marriage act (called "impotence"), that marriage could be declared *Ratum non Consummatum*. This is to say that even though the "exchange of vows" *(ratum)* was legally and properly done, the fulfillment of the vows by sexual union (*consummatum*) was impossible. The marriage was *non-consummatum*—"not consummated"—and hence not completed.

Therefore, after proper adjudication in a Church tribunal, the Pope could dissolve such a marriage. Then, each party—provided he or she is not *permanently* impotent—would be eligible to enter into another marriage.

A somewhat similar situation *may* also occur, even without impotence, when a couple *de facto* does not consummate their marriage. Such a non-completed marriage is valid, but not absolutely indissoluble and for a just cause may be dissolved by the Pope. There were a few *Ratum non Consummatum* cases on record during World War II. *Hypothetical case:* In 1943, a Catholic girl in Chicago marries her sweetheart who is serving in the Armed Forces. All arrangements for the wedding, such as filling out the required forms, obtaining the license and the necessary permissions, are done through the mail.

On the wedding day, the groom is able to obtain only a two-hour pass from his army camp. He arrives just in time for the ceremony, exchanges vows, kisses the bride and then hurries out of church to catch the next bus back to camp. She waves good-bye from the top of the church steps.

The newly-wedded recruit never gets back to his bride. He is shipped overseas for three years. During that time, the bride realizes that she made a mistake. She may apply for a *Ratum non Consummatum* dissolution, and it is likely that she would obtain it. Proof of the "non-consummation" could easily be obtained.

The Physical Union Is God-given.

We mention the above case, which is obviously exceptional, because we want people to realize that the sexual union is more than an *accessory* to marriage. Rather, it is *intrinsic* to it—one of the elements essential to its indissolubility. All false puritanical ideas should be put out of one's mind. The correct attitude must be that the physical union of husband and wife and the pleasure attendant to it are God-given, beautiful and desirable within marriage.

When God the Father created the human race, His infinite wisdom divided mankind into male and female: two different genders, two different sexes, each purposely created with distinctive physical differences. These physical differences are so ordained as to work together, to interact with each other. Why? To propagate the human race, to provide for the offspring and to deepen the bond between the parents.

Our bodies, and every part of them, are "good" in themselves, since they proceed from the hand of the infinitely perfect Being. It should be self-evident that these bodies of ours must be used only according to

God's purpose, God's plan. Thus, we must conform our behavior to the Divine Law as expressed in the Natural Law and in Church teaching. If our human nature—body and soul—conforms itself to God's will, the physical aspects of marriage will always be beautiful and holy.

DIFFICULTIES

Sometimes, one of the spouses refuses to see the physical and sexual side of marriage as God-given. This false view is usually not evident during courtship and engagement, and possibly even during the honeymoon and early years of marriage. But often the passing of years will change a person's view on this, and difficulties will emerge. Prior to their wedding day, the desire to consummate their union may have been so intense as to constitute a source of temptation. It may have required much prayer and self-discipline to avoid falling into sin. The young man and young woman could hardly wait to be physically joined with the blessing of the Sacrament.

But, to be sure, the months and years have added up: "We tend to take each other for granted. We know each other so thoroughly now—each other's moods, faults, and mannerisms. And besides, we are always busy or tired. After all, there are babies to care for and work to be done. There is not the same magic as when we were first married." Sometimes a wife who once was so anxious to consummate her marriage will now look upon marital intimacy as a "task," a duty to be performed and endured, and deep down she may have a semi-wish that her husband would not bother her with this.

Why does this happen? Why are there difficulties?

Factors

1. Puritanical Tendencies

As young boys and girls grow up, they live in a secular society that thrusts illicit sex into their faces at every turn. In a good home, in a good parish, among good teachers, they are taught (rightly) that sexual activity *outside of marriage* is evil and sinful, and it is prohibited by God for many good reasons.

But, often these instructions are imbalanced or incomplete. Sex is always understood to be "dirty," as are certain parts of our anatomy associated with it. As a youngster, perhaps your hand was slapped for touching the private parts of your body.

To offset any idea that "sex is dirty," a saintly priest of our acquaintance, who once taught moral theology at Seton Hall University, would begin his chapter on The Sixth Commandment in this way:

He would print in large letters on a blackboard the word "SEX." Naturally, the students perked up immediately. Then, he would point to the word and say: "Every one of you boys came into this world because of an act of SEX *on the part of your father and mother.* So, henceforth, don't any of you dare to ever think that SEX is evil or dirty. It is *good* and *beautiful*—provided that it is exercised within the laws of God."[7]

---

7. The reason why there are regulations and prohibitions regarding the use of the sexual faculty is not that it is "dirty," unclean or impure, but rather that it is *sacred*. In some respects, the situation is similar to regulations governing the reception of Holy Communion.

2. Wrong Ideas about Modesty

During one's adolescent years, most parental directions regarding modesty take the form of *negative* admonitions: "Don't do this. Don't do that."

God knows that we certainly need to be warned about the dangers lurking in the world—in movies, on T.V., in clothing styles, in rock music, in magazines, etc. Our virtue is attacked on every side, and to be sure, many teenagers are *not* admonished strongly enough to avoid the temptations surrounding them.

Parents, clergy and teachers, without a doubt, must repeat over and over the need for the children under their care to be wary of the dangers to holy purity and the necessity to flee from all near occasions of this sin.

But this approach is only *half* of the battle. We should show young Catholics that "virtue" means strength and beauty and happiness. We must remind them that it requires love and courage to imitate the admirable purity of the Saints. Let us give our idealistic and malleable youths the *positive* example of Our Blessed Mother, as well as St. Joseph, St. Anthony and St. Therese.

A famous convert, G. K. Chesterton, once wrote: "It is the obligation of all Christians to be *happy*."

Only the practice of true virtue will bring a deep, abiding happiness. On the other side of the coin, lack of virtue—immodesty and impurity—results in misery and a lessening of man's noble stature.

Our bodies were created by God for many purposes, one of which is the procreation of life. We must preserve the body and its reproductive functions for the day when we can present it to a beloved spouse in marriage. Our sexual function (which is, as we said, God-given and sacred) must be preserved like a precious diamond, so that someday it may be brought unblemished to the marriage bed.

Just *how* beautiful is the God-given intimacy of husband and wife? It has been compared to the miracle of the Holy Eucharist, that is, to the Real Presence of the Body and Blood of Jesus Christ:

> a. The Holy Eucharist is kept behind the locked doors of the tabernacle in a gold ciborium, on pure white linen. Only the priest, with his anointed hands, has the right to touch and distribute the Hosts. And why is this so? What is the result? An increase of *love* . . . between Our Lord and His people.

> b. The husband is in effect, the "priest" of his wife's body. He *alone* has the right to touch it . . . not because he is altogether worthy, but because he is "ordained," as it were, through the Sacrament of Matrimony. What results through this intimacy? An increase of love between himself and his spouse.

> *Conclusion:* Marital intimacy can and should be compared to the intimacy between the ordained priest and the Body and Blood of Our Saviour. According to St. Thomas Aquinas, an act of marital union, under the proper circumstances, is a source of grace.

3. Failure of Women to Enjoy Physical Intimacy

This syndrome is somewhat common to couples who have been married for a length of time. One or both (most often the woman) merely "puts up" with the marriage act, and secretly wishes that her partner would not request it. Why?

> a. A woman's psychology differs from that of a man. She looks upon the *sum total* of her

husband's actions as a preparation for physical union. If she is dissatisfied with some aspect of the total picture, she tends to be cool to his ardor.

b. Nervousness and tiredness.

c. Unwillingness to forgive hurts.

d. Old wives' tales, rumors, false information, bad advice from another unhappy woman, the influence of the feminist agenda, etc.

NOTE: Very often one partner (most often the male) is somewhat inconsiderate by not taking into account the different female psychology. Men can be very thoughtless, not out of malice, but rather out of ignorance.

4. Fears

a. *Before Marriage:* Sometimes listening to the bad advice of disgruntled and unhappily married people can generate fear of marriage. Sometimes the beauty and sacredness of marital intimacy is destroyed by repeated exposure to pornography and vulgar jokes.

b. *After Marriage*: God has made it possible that an act of physical love will result in conception. This is one of the greatest realities of all God's creation. But wicked, ignorant and illusioned people have so well broadcast their misunderstandings, their bad experiences, and their poor results in having and raising children that they have inculcated many fears in the minds of those just entering or still new to the married state. The result is that a number of fears over having children often are built up in people's minds. The following are some of the major fears.

1. Fear of Pregnancy

The secular-humanistic world looks upon conception as "bad luck"—an unfortunate consequence that must be avoided.

Sometimes we overhear people making denigrating remarks about "adding to the population." The myth of overpopulation[8] has created a situation in which some pregnant women are hesitant to appear in public. They may even fear to be seen in the supermarket because it is obvious to all that they are "in a family way."

One such mother, a beautiful Irish immigrant girl who was expecting her fifth child, cried to my own mother because of little comments she heard some of her neighbors make. My own mother, who gave blessed birth to nine children, assured the young Irish woman to be strong, "and tell those gossipy neighbors to go jump in the lake."

After all, according to the Bible, children are a great blessing and are to be cherished because they are all sent from the Creator Himself.

No doubt about it, pregnancy causes some suffering and inconvenience; it curtails freedom; it might necessitate quitting an outside job; maternity clothing may need to be purchased; medically, it may result in temporary backache or nausea.

Of course, all of these inconveniences are gladly to be endured for the sake of God and because new immortal souls have come into being. "Where there is love, there is no labor," says the great St. Augustine.

---

8. It is impossible for the world to be overpopulated. An all-wise God is both the Author of life and of the amount of space in the world to accommodate it. He knows what He is doing! Someone has calculated that if all the people in the world were crammed into the state of Texas, each one would have a city block to himself, the rest of the world remaining empty.

2. Fear of Another Child

It gets more and more difficult to raise children in the Catholic Faith and imbue them with Catholic morals in a world gone crazy with secularism and characterized by periodic economic fluctuations that generate feelings of insecurity. We have God's grace to aid us, however, and we have the reward of a life with purpose and a guarantee of eternity.

For the faint-hearted and for the non-believer, however, love-making becomes a snare and a delusion. An unholy attitude often develops that says, "We may have to pay for this," referring to the possible conception of a child. Sometimes the "we-are-taking-a-gamble" attitude—similar to Russian Roulette—dominates their lives and deprives them of God-given joy.

3. Fear of Human Criticism

If a couple is blessed with a large family, some of the wife's friends . . . yes, even her blood relatives (to their shame), may regard her as "You poor thing!" To those who do not have her motherly graces, changing diapers and getting up in the wee hours of the morning may seem like an unbearable burden.

NOTE: God's Providence always provides us with the grace, the strength and the good cheer to do what He asks us to do within our vocation.

4. Economic Worries

Money! Money! Money!

Thank God that our immigrant parents and grandparents did not let the lack of money prevent them from having many children. These men and women of faith opened their hearts to God. To them their *children* were their treasure.

Yet modern couples, who possess *ten times* as many conveniences and luxuries as their ancestors, often fear that they cannot afford any more children. "After all, we have the expenses of food, mortgage, automobile and clothing" . . . *and dinners out and cocktails and travel, it might be added!* In other words, they are confusing necessities with luxuries.

NOTE: The secret is *to live within your budget.* If the income does not match your social aspirations, then accept a *lower* socio-economic status.

But, *mirabile visu!*—"wonderful to see"—somehow or other, we never go "broke" having children. *God does indeed provide.* Yes! It takes faith and trust, fortified by daily prayer and at least weekly Mass and Holy Communion to have the supernatural confidence that God will indeed provide. Plus, the generous, joyful, realistic good example of our traditional-minded Catholic friends can also help.

5. Housing

"But we only have a small apartment."

Please keep in mind: God *will* provide. You may be crowded, and the kids may sleep 3 or 4 to a room, but it is only *for a time.* All things are passing. Children grow up quickly, and then *they* should be expected, with their little jobs, to help augment the family income, if need be.

The normal approach to teaching children the value of money and how to handle their money prudently is to have them begin to pay for their own expenses when they start to earn money, especially the costs of clothing, tuition, pocket-money, transportation (busfare, a new bicycle or a used car), insurance, dental expenses, etc. In this way, the parents are both teaching their youngsters to be responsible for their own expenses, and at the same time, relieving the family budget of much of the expense of further supporting that child.

6. In-Laws and Parents

Sometimes, especially in our modern society, in-laws and parents will discourage a young couple from having children. But they are giving flawed advice when they say things such as: "Don't have children right away. Get settled, save a little money, and then have your family."

The Church teaches that couples should be so prepared for marriage that, when they do get married, they are *already* "settled." They should eagerly await and pray for children as soon as God will send them. Bringing new souls into the world and caring for them is, after all, the *primary purpose* of marriage.

What a crime when parents of the expectant couple—parents who should be leading by example—actually make their grown children *uncomfortable* when it comes time for them to announce that they are "expecting." It is a sin of *blasphemy,* an insult to the all-provident God, the Creator of this arrangement for having children and the Provider of the grace to meet our every need in life. Such people betray the fact that their judgment has been overcome by the world and its short-sighted philosophy. They are to be pitied! *May God have mercy on them! May He enlighten their darkened minds!*

How beautiful are those prospective grandparents who rejoice and enthuse at the news of every "blessed event!" These are people of faith, and God will reward them for encouraging life. Young couples who are bearing children benefit in a hundred ways from faith-filled parents. Their love and encouragement is a gift from God.

REMEDIES

A. Intelligent Discussion of Problems

Husband and wife should be able to talk to each other like two grown-up friends. Intelligent, Christian communication is always beneficial on subjects such as:

1. Children: the possibility of their being conceived; their reason for existence.
2. God's purpose for all of us.
3. Human frailties.
4. The need to be guided by the Supreme Being, that is, by God and His Holy Church.

Here, we can clearly see the advantage of marrying one of our own kind. Couples should share the same faith and the same moral outlook on life.

Granted, young people in seeking a mate are tempted to place priority on good looks, financial achievement (or potential) and social status. This obsession with beauty and superficiality is unfortunate. Many good-looking, well-heeled social climbers are selfish, possess no genuine faith and have many problems within their psychological make-up.

During courtship, selfishness is often camouflaged. But after the wedding vows, the "real" person emerges from the disguise.

Example: A young girl, moderately attractive, meets a strikingly handsome guy. In addition to good looks, he has personality. He also knows how to dress and seems always to be on the go, doing interesting things. "Wow! What a *catch!* And he who could capture any girl in the world has picked *me,* an average-looking girl, to be his bride.

"*Now*, five years have passed, five years of his philandering and my always wondering where he is, a man who doesn't even want to talk to me and who is so selfish I could scream. O Lord, help me!"

If your marriage partner possesses the genuine, true, balanced Catholic Faith, you can be sure that you have married a person who will make a loyal, unselfish spouse and a loving, dependable parent. These are the qualities that will endure.

When it comes to the intelligent discussion of problems, unselfish and faith-filled couples will always have common grounds on which to discuss their problems. *Things can always be worked out.*

But, if one partner is selfish, worldly and shallow, it is heartbreaking for the good partner! The worldly spouse thinks from completely different premises. The good spouse reasons from a *God-centered* life; whereas, the worldly spouse works from a *"man-centered"* view of himself (or herself) and the world.

B. Understanding the Difference in the Sexes

1. Man's Love Is More Physical:

By nature, the male is more *active* than passive. He is the aggressive one: he whistles at the girls, he asks for dates. In marriage, the male most often initiates the fulfillment of the marriage act.

The physical and psychological make-up of the male—as well as his active tendencies—are all the product of God's wisdom and power. Our Creator made man this way.

Unfortunately, this natural, God-given tendency can be misdirected, exaggerated and abused. Pornographic magazines and sensuous films are aimed primarily at a male audience. Why? Because the secular media realizes that male passions are easily aroused by these stimuli.

A woman's passions are not affected in the same way.

2. Woman's Love Is More Emotional:

By nature, the female wants attention, affection

and security. Therefore, in order to acquire these things from the male, she takes pains to make herself attractive. As proof of this, consider the billions of dollars spent annually on cosmetics and ladies' fashions to achieve this end!

In marriage, women also desire the physical act of intimacy, but they are less likely to make it a priority. What a wife truly desires is affection and kindness, and she looks upon these things as *preparation* for the marital union.

NOTE: Many husbands do not understand this side of the female nature. They falsely reason that even though the husband may be cool, distant, and even outright mean-spirited, that when he seeks passionate love-making, his wife should share the same ardor. The man fails to recognize that the woman looks upon the physical union as the *culmination* of *many acts* of thoughtfulness. She does not *isolate* intimacy from the rest of their work-a-day life together.

3. Each Must Be Unselfish:

The consideration of each other's needs and desires is the goal of *really good* married people. True Christian love urges us to think of the other *first*. The husband should think of his wife first, and conversely, the wife should place her husband's wants ahead of her own.

The physical union should be inexorably bound up in their *caritas*—true Christian love—for each other, rather than separate and apart from it. That is what separates a loving relationship from mutual self-gratification.

4. The Importance of Daily Courtesies:

If there is real love and concern for each other, the physical union is *never* a source of trouble. Requests, as well as submission to requests, will all flow naturally, spontaneously and with ready co-operation. To facilitate this, each spouse should effortlessly extend little signs of affection each day: *For example,* a kiss in the morning; frequent, sincere compliments; thoughtful little gifts; a readiness to do favors.

NOTE: During the courtship, men usually act chivalrously. This is not done hypocritically, but with all sincerity and desire to show respect. Terms such as, "Please" and "Excuse me" are common. Doors are held open. A man stands when his wife-to-be enters the room. He holds her chair as she sits down.

But, alas! All too often, familiarity leads to neglect of these signs of respect, and the passage of a few months of marriage can see the disappearance of the gentleman and his thoughtfulness. *Men* tend to forget these small but meaningful expressions of affection and respect that they once exhibited.

A Personal Observation: My associate pastor and I often would stand on the front steps of our parish church observing various families arriving for Sunday Mass.

When a car with a man and a woman inside pulled up in front of church and the man parked the car and quickly hurried around to open the passenger-side door for the woman sitting there, we would whisper quietly to each other, "Obviously, they are not married!"

5. A Positive Attitude toward Children:

Our Catholic Faith teaches us that each child is a gift from God, a treasure, a blessing!

Couples should keep in mind that the *primary* purpose of the marital act is to open the door to God's creative power.

a. If the notion of conceiving a child is *excluded,* spiritual satisfaction is lost. The physical union descends into the merely carnal, resulting in many unhappy and broken marriages.

Statistics illustrate the fact that the more children a couple has, the less is the probability that they will separate or divorce.

b. Happiness in this world comes only after honestly facing reality as God made it. Married people should accept God's will with regard to sending children and rely upon His graces that they will be able to handle the job and the expense of raising them. This is the only way to live.

Without faith and trust in God and His plan, worry and concern for the future will always exist, and such worry is always non-productive. Our loving God will never give us more of a burden or allow us to suffer more temptation than we can handle. "My grace is sufficient for thee." (*2 Cor.* 12:9).

c. The possibility of conceiving a child makes lovemaking within the framework of marriage exciting and important. Will God now perform the miracle of creation? And if He does, what will the child be like? What great things will this newborn baby accomplish for God and for souls? Will we be the parents of a St. Therese or a St. Anthony?

What immense possibilities God has given us!

d. The value of children and the joy of having them is the *best publicity* for the institution of marriage.

e. Married couples should remember the following quote from the Marriage ceremony (in the liturgical Ritual): "Dear Friends in Christ: As you know, you are about to enter into a union which is most sacred and most serious. By this union, God has given to man and woman a share in the greatest work of creation: the continuation of the human race . . . Sacrifice is usually difficult and irksome, but love can make it easy, and perfect love can make it a joy."

THE MORALITY OF SEXUAL PLEASURE

1. Morality comes from God, from His Divine Essence. The task of His Church is to enunciate clearly this morality, always remembering that its

source is Our Creator Himself.

2. Human beings have free will. God requires that His Laws be observed, but He does not physically force compliance upon anyone.

Nevertheless, those who keep God's laws will be rewarded; whereas, those who refuse to keep His laws will be punished.

The Norms of Morality for Married Persons

Definitions: 1) "*complete* pleasure" means reaching climax; 2) "*incomplete* pleasure" means carnal arousal without reaching climax.[9]

1. Any act that does not prevent the semen from reaching its proper place is permitted.

By God's design, the semen is programmed to meet the ovum. It is morally wrong to frustrate this design, by placing the semen out of its proper place or by preventing ovulation.

Contraception (birth control) is always a mortal sin. This includes any pill, device, substance or any other means (by either the man or the woman) to prevent conception.[10] It also includes sterilization, such as vasectomy (in the male) or having the tubes tied—tubal ligation (in the female).

---

9. These definitions are part of traditional Catholic morality taught in priests' moral theology courses in the seminary.

10. Doctors and medical experts admit that birth control pills, implants and shots often work by causing a very early *abortion*, even if the woman is not aware this is happening. (The IUD operates by causing a very early abortion.) To take a chance on causing an abortion is a mortal sin in itself.
    Publisher's Note: Fortunately, a growing number of doctors have stopped prescribing contraceptives and abortifacient "contraceptives." See the book *Physicians Healed: Personal Stories of Fifteen Courageous Physicians Who Do Not Prescribe Contraception*, edited by Cleta Hartman (Dayton, OH: One More Soul, 1998).

NOTE: A sinful procedure or act is still a sin even if doctors or other medical persons insist that it is "necessary" or "must be done." God's law always comes first. (It is morally permitted to remove a reproductive organ that has a serious pathology, even though this would cause sterilization. Example: removal of a cancerous uterus.)

Also, the husband shares the responsibility for his wife's birth control (or abortion) if he consents to it, and the wife shares the responsibility for her husband's use of birth control if she consents to it.

2. Thoughts and desires about one's spouse entertained to stimulate sexual pleasure are not sinful, so long as they are thoughts and desires of lawful acts with one's spouse—and so long as they do not present the near occasion of mortal sin. (See point 3.)[11]

3. *Complete* satisfaction *apart* from one's spouse, i.e., *by oneself*, is always mortally sinful.

4. *Signs of affection,* either before the marital act or completely apart from it, are permitted and recommended.

5. Mutual actions which will result in *incomplete* pleasure are permitted, provided there is little or no danger of *"pollutio"* (i.e., "spilling the seed").

6. The *Debitum*—"marriage debt"—is a serious responsibility. If one spouse makes a "reasonable request" for marriage relations with the other, then the one requested has a serious obligation to comply. Otherwise, a refusal could lead to mortal sin on the part of the party that initiated the request. There-

---

11. May we recommend for Roman Catholic priests the book *Moral Theology* (18th edition), by Rev. Heribert Jone, O.F.M. Cap. (Imprimatur: Dec. 8, 1961 by John J. Wright, Bishop of Pittsburgh). TAN Books and Publishers, Inc., Rockford, Illinois, 1993. (See also St. Alphonsus Liguori's *Theologia Moralis.*)

fore, to refuse to honor the "marriage debt" is a mortal sin, unless there are sufficiently grave, overriding considerations.

Definitions:

1. *Debitum*: Literally: "debt." The debt—or obligation to allow marriage relations—which each spouse owes to the other by virtue of the marriage vow.

St. Paul wrote: "Let the husband render the debt to his wife, and the wife also in like manner to the husband. The wife hath not power of her own body, but the husband. And in like manner the husband also hath not power of his own body, but the wife. Defraud not one another, except, perhaps, by consent, for a time, that you may give yourselves to prayer; and return together again, lest Satan tempt you for your incontinency." (*1 Cor.* 7:3-5). (See also "Higher Spiritual Motives," p. 78.)

2. *Reasonable Request*: not contrary to right reason, as would be the case if, for example, the requesting party were completely intoxicated, abusive or extremely negligent of some necessary duty in marriage, or if the responding party suffered from serious illness.

In most cases, the request is reasonable, even if the requesting party is far from perfect, or if there have been marital disagreements. The person requested would be wrong to reject a spouse because of tiredness, or slight sickness, or headache, or as a tactic to get one's own way. Rejecting the request of one's spouse without a serious reason is a mortal sin. (The requesting party should keep in mind that it is good not always to insist on one's rights.)

Note: For an excellent explanation on the proper physical relationship between married persons, see St. Francis de Sales' classic *Introduction to the Devout Life,* Part III, chap. 39.

Further Moral Considerations

The use of contraceptives and abortifacients is contrary to the NATURAL LAW.

Natural Law is defined as "The laws of God which have been built into man's rational nature, i.e., into man's *soul*." All persons, no matter of what nationality or religion and even those of no religion, are bound by the Natural Law. (Examples of other offenses against the Natural Law are lying, stealing, murder and refusal to worship God.)

The Old Testament and New Testament, as well as the Church founded by Christ, have faithfully promulgated the Natural Law. Thus, Church teachings against abuses of the procreative faculties are not merely "Catholic rules." They are laws of Almighty God which apply to all people.

God Is the Author of the Marriage Act.

In addition to our knowledge that God is the Creator of all things, we intuitively recognize that God is the author of marital intimacy because of

1. *Its Beauty*—God's wondrous act of creation is perpetuated by this beautiful physical act of man and woman.

2. *Its Naturalness*—The uniting of the male and female bodies in marriage is natural, is not artificial. As long as it is *within* a legitimate marriage, it is the most perfect of all human unions.

3. *Its Pleasure*—The unique pleasure of the act of procreation is granted by God as an *enticement* to perpetuate the human race.'

This pleasure is also bestowed by God as a *reward* for the many hardships of married life and parenthood. According to Catholic theology, the *intensity of the pleasure* is a corroborative sign of God's encouragement.

4. *Its Holiness*—It can be compared to the Consecration at Holy Mass. In the Holy Sacrifice, the most pure Jesus Christ transforms earthly bread. At the Consecration, the bread is *elevated* to the highest plane and becomes a Source of holiness.

In the marital union, husband and wife come into contact with each other. Each one is elevated, so to speak, to a higher plane. Each one is sanctified by this union. It is indeed a source of holiness, a means of grace. Through this physical act, God gives graces, because this act is an *exercise* of the Sacrament of Matrimony.

5. *Its Psychological Purpose*—The marital act "isolates" two people from all other things. The world, with all its distractions, is left behind. For a precious few moments of time, the spouses possess "just each other." These moments may be compared to the moments a priest spends at Mass with the Body and Blood of Christ still present within him. He and Christ are one, isolated from all *worldly* concerns.

For a married couple, these moments of intimacy serve as a time when love is strengthened and refreshed, when their acceptance of each other is reaffirmed. It is a time to make up for arguments and slights and misunderstandings. It is the perfect way to say, *"I Love You!"*

CONCLUSION

Physical love is a *gift* of *God*. It is beautiful, natural, pleasurable, holy, mutually beneficial and productive. The happiness that God showers upon married people is a foreshadowing of the blessed happiness of Heaven.

Husband and wife must walk together down the road to eternal happiness. Thus, hand-in-hand and arm-in-arm, they will attain salvation *together.*

Appendix 1

PERIODIC CONTINENCE

Definition: To refrain from the marital union during the wife's fertile period during the month.

Teaching of the Roman Catholic Church

Periodic continence (periodic abstinence), for the purpose of limiting the chances for conception *is licit,* that is, morally allowed according to God's law and Catholic teaching, provided:

1. There is a *serious* reason. For example, grave health problems, serious economic reasons.
2. *Both* parties *mutually and freely agree* to the restrictions that it involves during the designated times.
3. There is no serious danger of sin for either party, especially sins of incontinence or other impurity.
4. That periodic continence be practiced only for the duration of time that the serious reason exists.

The practice of periodic continence should not bring with it a lessening of faith or trust in God's Wisdom.

Complete Surrender to the Will of God

The *ideal* in marriage is always to trust *completely* to God's Providence in the matter of bearing children. In other words, to accept *all* the children that God may send without reservation or question. If God cares

73

for "the birds of the air" and "the lilies of the field"
(*Matt.* 6:26, 28), then why should we lack trust in His
Providence? This complete surrender to the Will of God
does not necessarily mean that a couple will have a
large family. Abraham and Sara had one child, Isaac
and Rebecca had two children (twins).

Periodic Continence Is Morally Permitted

According to Jone's *Moral Theology* (#760, page 542):
"For a proportionate reason, and with mutual consent
of husband and wife, it is lawful intentionally to practice periodic continence, that is, restrict intercourse
to those times when conception is impossible."

NOTE: "Periodic continence" is a traditional Catholic
term and concept and should be used rather than
the term "natural family planning" (NFP), which refers
to a different concept and practice. The latter term
implies that the norm and the ideal is to "plan" one's
family; whereas, in Catholic moral teaching:

The *norm* (required) is to accept all the children
that God wants to send—with periodic continence
being morally permitted under the specified conditions cited above; and
The *ideal* (recommended but not required) is to
refrain from practicing periodic continence (even if
the couple fulfills the necessary conditions for it) and
simply to accept all the children that God wants to
send—or, heroically, to abstain completely (either for
a time, or for the rest of their marriage).

Note: The *Catechism of the Catholic Church* issued by the Holy
See in 1994 uses the term "periodic continence" (No. 2370). (It
does not use the term "natural family planning.")

Some Sacrifice Is Required

If all the moral conditions for periodic continence are verified, there remain three tasks:
1. Determine the fertile times with accuracy.
2. Practice voluntary self-control and mortification during those times.
3. Pray together that God's Will will be done and that your faith in the Church's teaching will remain constant.

To Determine the Fertile Times

Two sources of information are Liturgical Press (Billings method) and The Couple to Couple League (Sympto-Thermal method). (See pp. 79-80.)

Some Questions and Answers

Q. Are there abuses of periodic continence?

A. Yes. For example, when neo-Modernist dioceses sponsor education in "Natural Family Planning" (NFP), chances are that there will be lacking a proper and clear moral/doctrinal foundation, including the four requirements for legitimate practice of periodic continence. (See p. 73.)

All the U.S.A. dioceses teach harmful sex education in their school classrooms. Some sponsor a quasi-liberal lecturer who gives addresses on "Chastity" (so-called) to high school students. In these lectures, the instructors include information on NFP. Classroom sex education (termed "The Final Plague" by author Randy Engel) does great harm to students and actually leads Catholic children into sinful experimentation.

Q. Can periodic continence be misunderstood?

A. Certainly. A husband and wife may be too *scrupulous* and tend to consider the use of periodic continence as necessarily displeasing to God. If the proper conditions are fulfilled, couples are permitted, without pangs of conscience, to practice periodic continence. (See list of papal statements on pp. 78-79).

Q. How else may periodic continence be misunderstood?
A. By *indiscriminate* use. A couple may apply the "serious reason" condition to fit any and all reasons, including selfish ones.

Q. What safeguards will protect couples from abusing or misunderstanding periodic continence?
A. There are several ways:
1. Pray to know God's Will for you.
2. Seek the advice of a good priest.
3. Aspire to "complete surrender to Divine Providence." Pray for more trust in God and learn from the words of Christ: "But seek ye first the Kingdom of God and his justice, and all these things shall be added unto you." (*Luke* 12:31). "Be you therefore perfect, as also your heavenly Father is perfect." (*Matt.* 5:48). The Epistles of St. Paul, St. John and St. Jude constantly exhort us to sanctity, yes, even to *heroic* sanctity.

Q. What virtue, in particular, should married couples pray for?
A. For *trust*—trust in God's Providence. The great American saint, Mother Frances Xavier Cabrini, instructed her sisters that when things looked difficult, they should consider it an opportunity to *trust God more*. "*Tanto, Tanto, Tanto!*" she exclaimed— "More, More, More!"

Q. Suppose *one* spouse in the marriage lacks faith and trust and cannot seem to accept the required crosses in the spirit of the Crucifix and Church teaching? Furthermore, what if, because of this weakness, there arise conflicts and tensions in the marriage?

A. The more enlightened partner must firmly but quietly adhere to Catholic morals and Catholic norms. (Good principles will always win out in the end). Always show understanding and kindness toward the weaker spouse, just as Jesus Christ manifested compassion on those who faltered because of weakness. Our Saviour was more severe on those who acted out of malice or deliberate ignorance.

Q. What else should the stronger spouse do?

A. Give good example; be well-balanced; be dutiful and generous and cheerful in all aspects of home life.

Q. Anything else?

A. Yes. Pray together. Fr. Patrick Peyton's motto, "The family that prays together stays together," refers not only to non-separation, but to a wonderful unity of souls under God's just and mysterious Providence.

St. Paul wrote: "For when I am weak, then am I strong." (*2 Cor.* 12:10). He turned the recognition of his own weakness into an opportunity to *depend more on God,* and less on self. His own human deficiencies thereby became an occasion of grace.

This is a great lesson for those spouses who feel they are lacking in sufficient faith or trust in God.

For Our Edification

Many great saints were born because their holy parents trusted totally in God's wisdom. To name a few:

1) St. Catherine of Siena, often called the greatest woman in Christendom, was a twin and the 24th of 25 children.

2) St. Ignatius Loyola, founder of the Jesuits, was the last of 13 children.

3) St. Frances Xavier Cabrini, the great missionary to America, was a 13th child.

4) St. Therese the Little Flower was the last of nine children. She was born after her mother had lost three babies. St. Therese was called "the greatest saint of modern times" by Pope St. Pius X.

How blessed in Heaven are these parents who opened their arms to each other and their hearts to God! What countless graces have come into the world because of their faith and courage in accepting the children God wanted to send them!

Higher Spiritual Motives

Voluntary abstinence has been practiced for ascetic reasons throughout the Christian ages. Many devout Catholic couples have mutually resolved, as an act of penance and mortification, to forego the pleasures of physical intimacy for a time, such as during Lent or Advent, or even for their entire marriage. Indeed, Church history records a number of canonized saints who made resolutions of this nature.

Sources of Catholic Teaching

Documents of the Magisterium of the Roman Catholic Church (a partial listing) in which periodic continence is approved, either implicitly or explicitly:

March 2, 1853—Response *Non esse Inquietandos*— (Sacred Penitentiary).

June 16, 1880—Response repeated *Non esse Inquietandos*—(S.P.)

Dec. 31, 1931—Pius XI, Encyclical *Casti Connubii.*

Oct. 29, 1951—Pius XII, Address to Midwives.

Nov. 26, 1951—Pius XII, Address to Family Congress.

May 15, 1961—John XXIII, Encyc. *Mater et Magistra.*
June 23, 1964—Paul VI, Allocution to Cardinals.
July 25, 1968—Paul VI, Encyclical *Humanae Vitae.*
Nov. 3, 1979—John Paul II, Address to CLER and
    IFFLP.
Jan. 26, 1980—John Paul II, Address to Midwives.

NOTE: Pope Pius XII recommended that medical science employ some of its expertise, not in inventing immoral devices and procedures, but rather in determining with greater accuracy the woman's fertility cycle.

Books That May Be Helpful

NOTE: Books on "Natural Family Planning" are recommended here only as resources for determining the woman's fertile time each month—and not for all aspects of the philosophy of marriage which they may promote.

The following book is available from:

Liturgical Press
P.O. Box 7500
Collegeville, MN 56321
Tel. (320) 363-2213
800-858-5450

Natural Family Planning: The Ovulation Method, by John Billings, M.D. Step-by-step explanation of the Billings Method of determining the fertile times (based on the mucous symptom), with daily charts and stickers. 35 pages $5.95

The following book is available from:

Couple to Couple League
P.O. Box 111184
Cincinnati, Ohio 45211-1184
Tel. (513) 471-2000
Orders 800-745-8252

The Art of Natural Family Planning (4th Edition), by John F. Kippley and Sheila K. Kippley. How to determine the fertile time each month (based on the mucous symptom plus waking temperature), arguments opposing contraception, explanation and defense of breast feeding, return of fertility after childbirth, religious and moral aspects, effects on the marriage, many other related topics.
511 pages $19.95

Appendix 2

REFLECTIONS

1. "Charity[1] is patient, is kind: charity envieth not, dealeth not perversely; is not puffed up; is not ambitious, seeketh not her own, is not provoked to anger, thinketh no evil; rejoiceth not in iniquity, but rejoiceth with the truth; beareth all things, believeth all things, hopeth all things, endureth all things." (*1 Cor.* 13:4-7).

2. "Marriage may be said to be the nursery of mankind. Marriage shows that men are in some way immortal. A father dies without dying, for he lives again in his son and in all his descendants."
—Le Père Cordier (died 1695)

3. "When there is trouble in a marriage, if the fault-finding and nagging on the part of the wife would end, almost without exception will the problems lessen. It has happened even in the case of alcoholism. There is something *magical* about *silence* on the part of a wife. After all, she has the Rosary, doesn't she?"   —A Catholic Housewife

4. "If the *head* of the house sees himself relied upon in matters of worldly importance, the wife [when she is the only Catholic spouse] will find in him a

---

1. The Latin *caritas* is properly translated as "charity," in the sense of "supernatural love" or "Christian love."

81

more receptive partner whenever she has to lead in religious and moral matters. If he sees *himself as head,* he recognizes *her as heart* of the home.

"The children straighten out, are more cheerful; more gets accomplished. A husband who feels accepted and deferred to as 'head' becomes very earnest in his willingness to please."   —A Catholic Mother

Appendix 3

PRAYER TO THE
MOST SACRED HEART OF JESUS
TO BE SAID BY MARRIED
PEOPLE ON THEIR OWN BEHALF

O MOST SACRED HEART of Jesus, King and center of all hearts, dwell in our hearts and be our King. Grant us by Thy grace to love each other truly and chastely, even as Thou hast loved Thine immaculate Bride, the Church, and didst deliver Thyself up for her.

Bestow upon us the mutual love and Christian forbearance that are so acceptable in Thy sight, and a mutual patience in bearing each other's defects, for we are certain that no living creature is free from them. Permit not the slightest misunderstanding to mar that harmony of spirit which is the foundation of that mutual assistance in the many and varied hardships of life, to provide which woman was created and united inseparably to her husband.

Grant, O Lord God, that between us there may be a constant and holy rivalry in striving to lead a perfect Christian life, by virtue of which the divine image of Thy mystic union with Holy Church, imprinted upon us on the happy day of our marriage, may shine forth more and more clearly. Grant, we beseech Thee, that our good example of Christian living may be a source of inspiration to our children, to spur them on to conform their lives also to Thy holy Law. And finally, after this exile, may we be found worthy, by the help of Thy grace, for which we earnestly pray, to ascend into Heaven, there to be joined with our children forever, and to praise and bless Thee through everlasting ages. Amen.

NOTE: If they have no children, instead of the words: "Grant, O Lord God, etc. . . . Amen," let them pray as follows:

Grant, O Lord God, that between us there may be a constant and holy rivalry in our efforts to lead a truly Christian life, by virtue of which the divine image of Thy mystic union with Thy Holy Church, which Thou didst deign to impress upon us on the happy day of our marriage, may shine forth more and more clearly; and so living, may we, both of us, ascend into Heaven and be found worthy to praise Thee and bless Thee forever. Amen.

(*Raccolta*, no. 769. An indulgence of 300 days was originally granted for the devout recitation of this prayer. —S.P. Ap., Dec. 11, 1923 and Nov. 25, 1936. A "partial" indulgence would be granted according to the new [1968] regulations on Indulgences.)

Saint Maria Goretti, Virgin and Martyr
1891-1902
She heroically chose death rather than commit sin.

If you have enjoyed this book, consider making your next selection from among the following . . .

Life Everlasting. *Garrigou-Lagrange, O.P.* 13.50
Mother of the Saviour/Our Int. Life. *Garrigou-Lagrange* 13.50
Three Ages/Int. Life. *Garrigou-Lagrange. 2 vol.* 42.00
Ven. Francisco Marto of Fatima. *Cirrincione*, comp. 1.50
Ven. Jacinta Marto of Fatima. *Cirrincione* 2.00
St. Philomena—The Wonder-Worker. *O'Sullivan* 7.00
The Facts About Luther. *Msgr. Patrick O'Hare* 16.50
Little Catechism of the Curé of Ars. *St. John Vianney.* 6.00
The Curé of Ars—Patron Saint of Parish Priests. *Fr. B. O'Brien.* 5.50
Saint Teresa of Avila. *William Thomas Walsh* 21.50
Isabella of Spain: The Last Crusader. *William Thomas Walsh* 20.00
Characters of the Inquisition. *William Thomas Walsh* 15.00
Blood-Drenched Altars—Cath. Comment. on Hist. Mexico. *Kelley* 20.00
The Four Last Things—Death, Judgment, Hell, Heaven. *Fr. von Cochem.* ... 7.00
Confession of a Roman Catholic. *Paul Whitcomb* 1.50
The Catholic Church Has the Answer. *Paul Whitcomb* 1.50
The Sinner's Guide. *Ven. Louis of Granada* 12.00
True Devotion to Mary. *St. Louis De Montfort* 8.00
Life of St. Anthony Mary Claret. *Fanchón Royer* 15.00
Autobiography of St. Anthony Mary Claret. 13.00
I Wait for You. *Sr. Josefa Menendez* .... .75
Words of Love. *Menendez, Betrone, Mary of the Trinity.* 6.00
Little Lives of the Great Saints. *John O'Kane Murray* 18.00
Prayer—The Key to Salvation. *Fr. Michael Müller.* 7.50
Passion of Jesus and Its Hidden Meaning. *Fr. Groenings, S.J.* 15.00
The Victories of the Martyrs. *St. Alphonsus Liguori* 10.00
Canons and Decrees of the Council of Trent. *Transl. Schroeder* 15.00
Sermons of St. Alphonsus Liguori for Every Sunday. 16.50
A Catechism of Modernism. *Fr. J. B. Lemius* 5.00
Alexandrina—The Agony and the Glory. *Johnston.* 6.00
Life of Blessed Margaret of Castello. *Fr. William Bonniwell.* 7.50
The Ways of Mental Prayer. *Dom Vitalis Lehodey* 14.00
Catechism of Mental Prayer. *Simler* 2.00
St. Francis of Paola. *Simi and Segreti.* 8.00
Abortion: Yes or No? *Dr. John L. Grady, M.D.* 2.00
The Story of the Church. *Johnson, Hannan, Dominica.* 16.50
Reign of Christ the King. *Davies* 1.25
Hell Quizzes. *Radio Replies Press* 1.50
Indulgence Quizzes. *Radio Replies Press* 1.50
Purgatory Quizzes. *Radio Replies Press* 1.50
Virgin and Statue Worship Quizzes. *Radio Replies Press* 1.50
The Holy Eucharist. *St. Alphonsus* 10.00
Meditation Prayer on Mary Immaculate. *Padre Pio* 1.50
Little Book of the Work of Infinite Love. *de la Touche.* 3.00
Textual Concordance of The Holy Scriptures. *Williams* 35.00
Douay-Rheims Bible. *Leatherbound* 35.00
The Way of Divine Love. *Sister Josefa Menendez* 18.50
The Way of Divine Love. (pocket, unabr.). *Menendez.* 8.50
Mystical City of God—Abridged. *Ven. Mary of Agreda* 18.50

Prices subject to change.

Moments Divine—Before the Blessed Sacrament. *Reuter* 8.50
Miraculous Images of Our Lady. *Cruz* 20.00
Miraculous Images of Our Lord. *Cruz* 13.50
Raised from the Dead. *Fr. Hebert* 16.50
Love and Service of God, Infinite Love. *Mother Louise Margaret* 12.50
Life and Work of Mother Louise Margaret. *Fr. O'Connell* 12.50
Autobiography of St. Margaret Mary 6.00
Thoughts and Sayings of St. Margaret Mary 5.00
The Voice of the Saints. *Comp. by Francis Johnston* 7.00
The 12 Steps to Holiness and Salvation. *St. Alphonsus* 7.50
The Rosary and the Crisis of Faith. *Cirrincione & Nelson* 2.00
Sin and Its Consequences. *Cardinal Manning* 7.00
Fourfold Sovereignty of God. *Cardinal Manning* 5.00
Dialogue of St. Catherine of Siena. *Transl. Algar Thorold* 10.00
Catholic Answer to Jehovah's Witnesses. *D'Angelo* 12.00
Twelve Promises of the Sacred Heart. (100 cards) 5.00
Life of St. Aloysius Gonzaga. *Fr. Meschler* 12.00
The Love of Mary. *D. Roberto* 8.00
Begone Satan. *Fr. Vogl* 3.00
The Prophets and Our Times. *Fr. R. G. Culleton* 13.50
St. Therese, The Little Flower. *John Beevers* 6.00
St. Joseph of Copertino. *Fr. Angelo Pastrovicchi* 6.00
Mary, The Second Eve. *Cardinal Newman* 3.00
Devotion to Infant Jesus of Prague. *Booklet* .... .75
Reign of Christ the King in Public & Private Life. *Davies* 1.25
The Wonder of Guadalupe. *Francis Johnston* 7.50
Apologetics. *Msgr. Paul Glenn* 10.00
Baltimore Catechism No. 1 .... 3.50
Baltimore Catechism No. 2 .... 4.50
Baltimore Catechism No. 3 .... 8.00
An Explanation of the Baltimore Catechism. *Fr. Kinkead* 16.50
Bethlehem. *Fr. Faber* 18.00
Bible History. *Schuster* 13.50
Blessed Eucharist. *Fr. Mueller* 9.00
Catholic Catechism. *Fr. Faerber* 7.00
The Devil. *Fr. Delaporte* 6.00
Dogmatic Theology for the Laity. *Fr. Premm* 20.00
Evidence of Satan in the Modern World. *Cristiani* 10.00
Fifteen Promises of Mary. (100 cards) 5.00
Life of Anne Catherine Emmerich. 2 vols. *Schmoeger* 37.50
Life of the Blessed Virgin Mary. *Emmerich* 16.50
Manual of Practical Devotion to St. Joseph. *Patrignani* 15.00
Prayer to St. Michael. (100 leaflets) 5.00
Prayerbook of Favorite Litanies. *Fr. Hebert* 10.00
Preparation for Death. (Abridged). *St. Alphonsus* 8.00
Purgatory Explained. *Schouppe* 13.50
Purgatory Explained. (pocket, unabr.). *Schouppe* 9.00
Fundamentals of Catholic Dogma. *Ludwig Ott* 21.00
Spiritual Conferences. *Tauler* 13.00
Trustful Surrender to Divine Providence. *Bl. Claude* 5.00
Wife, Mother and Mystic. *Bessieres* 8.00
The Agony of Jesus. *Padre Pio* 2.00

Prices subject to change.

Sermons of the Curé of Ars. *Vianney* 12.50
St. Antony of the Desert. *St. Athanasius* 5.00
Is It a Saint's Name? *Fr. William Dunne* 2.50
St. Pius V—His Life, Times, Miracles. *Anderson* 5.00
Who Is Therese Neumann? *Fr. Charles Carty.* 2.00
Martyrs of the Coliseum. *Fr. O'Reilly.* 18.50
Way of the Cross. *St. Alphonsus Liguori* 1.00
Way of the Cross. *Franciscan version* 1.00
How Christ Said the First Mass. *Fr. Meagher* 18.50
Too Busy for God? Think Again! *D'Angelo* 5.00
St. Bernadette Soubirous. *Trochu* 18.50
Passion and Death of Jesus Christ. *Liguori* 10.00
Treatise on the Love of God. 1 Vol. *St. Francis de Sales* 24.00
Confession Quizzes. *Radio Replies Press* 1.50
St. Philip Neri. *Fr. V. J. Matthews.* 5.50
St. Louise de Marillac. *Sr. Vincent Regnault* 6.00
The Old World and America. *Rev. Philip Furlong* 18.00
Prophecy for Today. *Edward Connor* 5.50
The Book of Infinite Love. *Mother de la Touche* 5.00
Chats with Converts. *Fr. M. D. Forrest.* 10.00
The Church Teaches. *Church Documents* 16.50
Conversation with Christ. *Peter T. Rohrbach* 10.00
Purgatory and Heaven. *J. P. Arendzen.* 5.00
Liberalism Is a Sin. *Sarda y Salvany* 7.50
Spiritual Legacy of Sr. Mary of the Trinity. *van den Broek* 10.00
The Creator and the Creature. *Fr. Frederick Faber* 16.50
Radio Replies. 3 Vols. *Frs. Rumble and Carty* 42.00
Convert's Catechism of Catholic Doctrine. *Fr. Geiermann* 3.00
Incarnation, Birth, Infancy of Jesus Christ. *St. Alphonsus* 10.00
Light and Peace. *Fr. R. P. Quadrupani* 7.00
Dogmatic Canons & Decrees of Trent, Vat. I. *Documents.* 9.50
The Evolution Hoax Exposed. *A. N. Field* 7.50
The Primitive Church. *Fr. D. I. Lanslots.* 10.00
The Priest, the Man of God. *St. Joseph Cafasso* 13.50
Blessed Sacrament. *Fr. Frederick Faber* 18.50
Christ Denied. *Fr. Paul Wickens* 2.50
New Regulations on Indulgences. *Fr. Winfrid Herbst* 2.50
A Tour of the Summa. *Msgr. Paul Glenn* 18.00
Spiritual Conferences. *Fr. Frederick Faber* 15.00
Latin Grammar. *Scanlon and Scanlon* 16.50
A Brief Life of Christ. *Fr. Rumble* 2.00
Marriage Quizzes. *Radio Replies Press* 1.50
True Church Quizzes. *Radio Replies Press.* 1.50
The Secret of the Rosary. *St. Louis De Montfort.* 5.00
Mary, Mother of the Church. *Church Documents* 4.00
The Sacred Heart and the Priesthood. *de la Touche* 9.00
Revelations of St. Bridget. *St. Bridget of Sweden* 3.00
Magnificent Prayers. *St. Bridget of Sweden* 2.00
The Happiness of Heaven. *Fr. J. Boudreau* 8.00
St. Catherine Labouré of the Miraculous Medal. *Dirvin* 13.50
The Glories of Mary. *St. Alphonsus Liguori* 16.50
The Three Ways of the Spiritual Life. *Garrigou-Lagrange, O.P.* 6.00

Prices subject to change.